UNEASILY IN LOVE WITH GOD

A collection of the writings of
the Reverend Dr. Herman F. Reissig

Bruce Hoskins, photographer

UNEASILY IN LOVE WITH GOD

HERMAN F. REISSIG
Pastor & Prophet

Selections from his sermons, articles, lectures,
prayers, letters and ruminations

Written and Edited by
his friends with the support and encouragement
of Florence Reissig

Two Bytes Publishing
Darien, Connecticut

ISBN: 1-881907-06-6 (soft cover edition)

Two Bytes Publishing
Darien, Connecticut

PRINTED IN THE UNITED STATES OF AMERICA

TABLE OF CONTENTS

Photographer unknown

"I do not want to be, nor ever need to be, retired from the task of trying to respect and love my fellow travelers, beginning with those nearest me."

EDITORS' FOREWORD

Those who prophesy speak to other people for their upbuilding and encouragement and consolation. Those who speak in a tongue build up themselves, but those who prophesy build up the church.

- I Corinthians 14:3

A group of friends and admirers of Herman Reissig with the support and encouragement of Florence Reissig, his wife of his last eleven years, felt that Herman's messages were too important to be forgotten. This memorial volume of selections from his writings -- sermons and prayers, addresses and essays, extracts from his book, *Man's New Home,* newspaper columns, letters to friends, and what he called "ruminations"" (his name for a page or two of reflection on a topic sent to several readers at once) -- is one result.

Herman Reissig served the First Congregational Church of Greenwich, in Old Greenwich, Connecticut for 13 years, first as Interim Pastor from 1972 to 1974, and then as Pastor Emeritus until his death in 1985. This volume is a memorial to a former pastor who was loved and respected for preaching that challenged us and for his life-long advocacy of Christian ethics and social action in the arena of public policy as well as in the church.

This book is published, not simply out of affection for a friend now gone from our midst, but because we believe that Herman was a true prophet, called by God to address this age as surely as Amos, Isaiah and Jeremiah were called to theirs. He still speaks a perennially relevant word, and that word should be heard more widely.

We hope that these writings, plus this remembrance of him as a person, will make new friends for him, and will be valued as a treasury of wisdom: insights he gained and shared with us through years of rapid change and social as well as theological turbulence. We want this especially for theological students in their formative years in the seminaries and for ministers in the field struggling to preach and act with prophetic power, offering a true word to a world in need. They need persuasive role models like Herman who challenged us all to intellectual rigor and honesty as well as courageous Christian action.

Readers should be aware that the friends and admirers responsible for this book were essentially in agreement with Herman's thinking on most of the issues presented. However, Herman also had extensive dialogues with those who disagreed with him. Persons critical of many of his statements still loved, respected and admired him because of his readiness to listen to contrary views and debate the issues.

This book is not a biography and the chapters are not in chronological order. They can be read sequentially or randomly. The pictures of Herman that precede the chapters depict him at that time in his life, and the captions are quotations from the chapters. The Appendices contain three full sermons and three segments from Herman's book *Man's New Home*. When sections from these sermons and book segments appear in the chapters, the reader is referred to the Appendices for the complete text.

Readers who knew Herman may want to write in response to this book. L. Alexander Harper has kindly volunteered to act as correspondent. He may be reached at 144 Gillies Lane, Norwalk, CT 06854. Telephone: (203) 857-0360.

ACKNOWLEDGMENTS

The Herman F. Reissig Memorial Committee responsible for sorting through Herman's voluminous files, selecting the material, and editing and publishing this book included:

Derek Boothby
L. Alexander Harper
R. Alan Johnson
Ruth and Richard Pope
Florence Reissig
Patty A. Tirana, Chairperson
Richard Vogt
Katherine Warren
Betty and Harry Woodman
Mary Lou Woods

The Committee particularly wishes to acknowledge the efforts of its Chairperson Patty Tirana in getting the project started and of Harry Woodman for compilation and editing responsibility; also thanks to: Carol Woodman for typing the manuscript, Sheila Johnson for the calligraphy and Elizabeth F. Clark, the publisher.

The Committee also wishes to acknowledge the contributions of the following persons whose generosity made publication possible:

Robert and Persis Alden
Derek and Catherine Boothby
Jerry Bradley
Carl and Nancy Brose
Walter Brueggemann
Theodosia Budington
Curtis and Joyce Carlson
Joan Cleworth
Frank Crabill
Deborah Dear
Vincent and Susan DeSimone
Hans Farman
Gary and Carol Farn
Martha Fingerle
George and Dorothy Fisk
Anne Fox
Naomi Geisswein
L. Alexander Harper
William and Allie Holmes
Jonathon Hunt
R. Alan Johnson
John and Mary Leinbach
Grace Newcomer
John and Barbara Norrgard
Kenneth and Erna Olson
Curvin O'Rielly
Richard and Ruth Pope
Florence Reissig

Harlan and Wendy Reynolds
Thomas and Brenda Stiers
Patty A. Tirana
Ferdinand and Cornelia Veith
Richard Vogt
Dwight and Katherine Warren
Jefferson and Jean Watkins
William and Karen Watt
Caralliene Westbrook
C. Webb and Sallie Williams
Robert and Marcia Wilson
Betty and Harry Woodman
Clifford Woods
Mary Lou Woods
Stanley and Helene Wright
Women's Fellowship
First Congregational Church of Greenwich

Finally, we thank the following for their permission to use excerpts from their material:

Christianity and Crisis, Inc., New York, New York
The Ledger, Lakeland, Florida
A.D. (Successor to *United Church Herald* and *Social Action*), United Church of Christ, Cleveland, Ohio
A Calendar of Prayer for the United Church of Christ: 1991-1992
Martha B. Porter, photographer, Sharon, Connecticut
Helen S. Allen, artist, Old Greenwich, Connecticut

UNITED CHURCH OF CHRIST + THAT THEY MAY ALL BE ONE +

Martha B. Porter, photographer

Herman Reissig's incisive mind, articulated values and firm conscience made his voice one to be reckoned with.

Chapter I. PASTOR AND PROPHET

By the Rev. L. Alexander Harper, Minister,
United Church of Christ

We no longer have, as past societies have had, any picture of individual Man (Stoic Philosopher, Christian Religious, Rational Gentleman) by which to recognize ourselves and against which to measure ourselves; we are anything. But if anything, then nothing, and it is not everyone who can live with that... He (Thomas More) became for me a man with an adamantine sense of his own self. He knew where he began and where he left off, what area of himself he could yield... At length he was asked to retreat from that final area where he located himself. And there this supple, humorous, unassuming and sophisticated person set like metal, was overtaken by an absolutely primitive rigor, and could no more be budged than a cliff.

-- Robert Bolt, A Man for All Seasons, preface, xi

A Man of Passion and Action

Playwright Robert Bolt's finely chiseled description of Sir Thomas More also fits well Herman Frederick Reissig (1899-1985), certainly for his last 25 years when I knew him. To be sure, Reissig was not beheaded for his stubborn conscience, as More was while Lord Chancellor to King Henry the Eighth. On second thought, there were controversies in which some might have gladly wielded the axe on Herman too!

What strikes me in Bolt's description as defining Reissig is "this supple, humorous, unassuming and sophisticated person" who yet had "an adamantine sense of his own self." Whether the issue was civil liberties or racial justice, the United Nations or U.S. policy on Latin America or the Soviet Union, Herman Reissig's incisive mind, articulated values and firm conscience made his voice one to be reckoned with. Yet his warmth and sly humor made him easy to be with, even in disagreement.

Most readers of this book -- former parishioners -- will probably not know the Herman Reissig of national, public controversy in his middle years, especially his important 17 years as Secretary for International Relations of the Council for Christian Social Action (CCSA), instrumentality of Congregational Christian Churches and later of the United Church of Christ (UCC). This book should expand their vision of this remarkable man of passion and action.

They remember "Dr. Reissig" simply as a pastor and friend, but one with backbone: he didn't just stand, he always stood for something. Most of these are members of First Congregational Church in Old Greenwich. Some knew him also as teacher from well-attended lectures and courses at the church.

Herman had been called out of retirement in Florida to help guide the church through an interim year or more while it sought a permanent new pastor. It was customary then for interim ministers to "coast" through such a period, preaching and teaching on tiptoe, as it were. They would glad-hand parishioners, call on the sick and elderly, but avoid at all cost wading into uncertain waters of controversy in church or community. "In interim preaching," said a cynical adage we both knew, "stick to the 23rd Psalm, the Lord's Prayer and First Corinthians 13: they can't offend anyone."

Herman would have none of this pussy-footing. He empowered us to avoid the molasses of being "all things to all men." We had to help the congregation to wrestle with painful, uncertain issues of the day in light of Christian faith, never dogmatically and always in dialogue rather than monologue. "The road to a church that really grapples with our human condition," Herman wrote later, "is long, narrow and hard, -- and few there will be that have the courage and faith to walk that road."

Reissig had a way with words; he made them dance with fresh meaning and delight. His were the letters you saved; his, the articles you clipped to re-read. His were the sermons you took to heart; his, the prayers that resonated with your own soul's longings and gave them voice. He had a healthy skepticism about the language of religious tradition -- outworn words, heavy with barnacles like an old ship, words like *atonement* ("If God made Jesus suffer for my sins, he'd be immoral!") and *invocation* ("Isn't God always present?"). Even the word *God*, said Herman, "has lost its juice."

In honoring honest doubt and searching for fresh language for religious reality, Herman made contact with skeptics galore. They took him seriously because he seemed more honest than most clerics who used conventional language and were "paid purveyors of foregone conclusions," as Herman called them. Into his 70s, he was a favorite counselor of rebellious teenagers in Lakeland, Florida, where he first retired. They sought him out as "one of them" in his respect for them as persons rather than "kids" and his shared skepticism about prissy proscriptions and pieties.

"I am, I guess it could be said, something of a dissenter," Herman wrote in 1983, "dissenting from traditional theological ideas and from orthodox political and economic views. It would be nice to be able to say that my dissents come straight from the Bible or from careful objective thinking, or from a combination of the two. It must, after all, be admitted that the Old Testament prophets and Jesus were famous dissenters from majority opinion. But this would mean giving myself too much credit."

Earlier Life

A sketch of Herman Reissig's earlier life may help give the truth of his utterances "a habitation and a home." He was born in 1899 in Farmington, New York, in the Finger Lakes region. He had a brother (also a Lutheran minister) and six sisters, all older than he. His sister Lucy wrote a little book about the family entitled *Seven, Eight, Shut the Gate*.

Herman's father, Friederich Ernst Reissig, fought in the Franco-Prussian War, was a machinist till the age of 30, when he entered a Missionary Seminary of the Church of the Brethren. At age 35 Ernst emigrated from Germany to America to be a pastor to rural Lutheran churches.

Herman attended Wagner College, then the Mt. Airy Lutheran Theological Seminary in Philadelphia, where he did his B.D. studies. He confessed to a friend years later: "I got along all right at the seminary, but the teachers were dully orthodox, not creative. So I did as little prescribed work as possible and read widely in non-prescribed books and went here and there looking for thinkers who challenged my mind and imagination." The faculty recommended this rebel's degree; trustees refused.

Late in his career Herman was honored with a Doctor of Divinity degree from Pacific School of Religion for his prophetic ministry. He also won several preaching prizes, both in earlier years and in the year of his death. His sermons had drawn high praise from such notables as Harry Emerson Fosdick of Riverside Church, Methodist Bishop Francis J. McConnell, and the second U.C.C. President, Avery Post.

His first wife, mother of his two children, had been Annette Beyer. Their sons are Daniel, a financial editor, and Richard, a professional musician; both work in New York. Herman's second wife, Frances Emerson Bradley, died in Old Greenwich in 1973. He subsequently married Florence DeFrees May, who survived him and lives in Portsmouth, New Hampshire.

Reissig served the Lutheran Church of the Good Shepherd in Brooklyn in the early 1920's. When his strict adherence to the Augsburg Confession (e.g. virgin birth, substitutionary atonement) was required, honesty compelled his resignation. His ordination was transferred to the theologically more permissive Congregational Churches in 1925.

That same year he became pastor of the West End Congregational Church in Bridgeport, Connecticut, in 1925, then a small "worker's church," as Herman called it. In 1930 he was called as pastor of the King's Highway Congregational Church in Brooklyn. He remembered it as "a middle-class church with lawyers, teachers and doctors."

Against Communism

In 1937 Herman Reissig was drawn to active participation in relief action for victims in the Spanish Civil War. He became executive of the Spanish Refugee Relief Campaign from 1937 to 1941. This proved a fateful decision. It thrust him professionally into the arena of public affairs. It also caused his embroilment in national controversy over "communist subversion." The cause of

Spanish Republicans attracted diverse enemies of Fascism and foes of the barbarisms of dictator Franco, allied with Hitler. When the Republican cause was lost, some 400,000 refugees streamed into France without food, money or medical care -- more than half of them women and children. Minimal aid was provided in refugee camps, basic support and medical care, financed by gifts from all over the world.

Supporters of aid for the refugees included Marxists, of course, among the sympathizers. Gifts to the consolidated Campaign (Herman helped to raise $1,000,000) enabled staff in France to reunite separated families and to provide survival aid in the wretched camps under French military supervision.

A leadership struggle developed in the Campaign between the communists and the non-communists, of whom Reissig was one. As the Campaign's CEO, Reissig was on the catbird seat. He was necessarily a part of many different appeals for refugee aid to Spanish Republicans. When communists were identified in the Campaign, others -- including Reissig -- were tarred with the same brush, especially by the notorious House Committee to Investigate Un-American Activities, chaired by Representative Martin Dies.

Reissig himself was cited twelve times in one report from Dies to the House of Representatives as a subversive if not actually a communist himself. While the report was highly inaccurate, reports in the press and the Congressional Record were electric in branding Reissig as a "dangerous radical." This reputation clung to him for almost 20 years. His church-sponsored addresses across the country were sometimes picketed by right-wing organizations on the strength of the remembered Dies report.

Shortly after the Dies Committee incident, it became clear that the communists were trying to use the Campaign largely to advance their own cause. Reissig initiated actions that led to the expulsion of all communists and their supporters. They formed a separate, rival organization and bitterly assailed Reissig. According to Reissig, the communists actually burglarized the complete files of the Campaign that were en route in a truck. These were never returned.

This bittersweet experience in Spanish refugee aid served Reissig in later prolific writings, addresses and workshops interpreting the rise of communism from his somewhat chastened, liberal perspective. These include his book, *Man's New Home*; an influential pamphlet, "How to Combat Communism"; together with a compelling indictment of the Dies Committee, "This Too Is Subversive!".

Social Action

After his experience in Spanish refugee aid, Reissig was called in 1941 to be pastor of the large First Union Congregational Church in Quincy, Illinois. While there he was President of the Quincy Council of Churches and a popular chapel speaker at midwestern colleges. Yet rising opposition, in what he called "this high society church," to his calls for justice for the dispossessed led to Reissig's resignation in 1947. He became for a year Field Secretary for the American Committee for the World Council of Churches.

In 1948 Reissig was called to be Director of International Relations in the Council for Christian Social Action of The Congregational Christian Churches, later the United Church of Christ. In this position he found an outlet for fullest expression of his theological ethics in analysis of world affairs and U. S. foreign policy.

Looking back on the experience two decades later, Reissig wrote: "No Christian should feel at home in this kind of world. Like those ancient Hebrews in Babylon, we are exiles... We must at least feel the tension, an almost agonizing tension between our religion and the way our world thinks and acts."

This helps to explain why he was haunted by the self-composed epitaph of poet Robert Frost: "I was uneasily in love with the world."

On the CCSA staff for seventeen years, Reissig wrote articles for *Social Action* (CCSA journal), *The United Church Herald* (UCC magazine), *Christianity and Crisis*, *The Christian Century* and other ecumenical journals. With consultants from the United Nations, the State Department and university faculties, he conducted scores of weekend workshops across the country, analyzing for church participants complex issues of international relations. I was his junior colleague on the denomination's national staff for Herman's last four years there.

Reissig led six study seminars to Europe, Africa and the Middle East. These were unusual in their interviews with key political leaders and in serious study, including advance preparation expected of participants. By the time of his mandatory retirement (by rule) from the CCSA in 1965, he had won an enviable reputation as a discerning, provocative writer and a leader in ethics and foreign affairs. Tributes to "Hi" Reissig were legion: from fellow ministers and ecumenical colleagues, religious editors, teachers of Christian ethics like Roger Shinn, and civil libertarians like Roger Baldwin, founder of the American Civil Liberties Union.

Strongly influenced by the political theology of Reinhold Niebuhr, Reissig was never a doctrinaire pacifist. Yet he wrote and spoke ominously of the "war system." It was fueled, he said, by a self-serving military-industrial complex, of which departing President Eisenhower had also warned. It was also fueled, he added, by the virulent anti-communism in this country long after the McCarthy era, and likely to yield a nuclear holocaust if unchecked.

In the year of his retirement from the CCSA staff, Reissig became interim minister of the United Church in Gainesville, Florida. Then he "retired" to Lakeland, Florida, only to become founder and first president of a Human Relations Council for Lakeland, an organization that fostered positive communication among races. His talents quickly recognized, he was also drafted onto the Executive Committee of the Polk County Migrant Ministry and the Florida Conference (UCC) Social Action Committee.

He became a regular columnist, with picture and byline, for the Lakeland *Ledger*. He was the guru of a group of activist clergy who met with him for inspiration. Yet he dared complain to me that he had "too little to do" in "this intellectual desert" of Florida retirees, who could play shuffleboard but not discuss important books.

First Congregational Church, Old Greenwich

In 1971 I had the most inspired hunch of my life. As interim senior minister of the First Congregational Church in Old Greenwich, I recommended that this church consider calling Herman as interim associate during the search for permanent leadership. Fully informed of his background, church officers interviewed him and promptly called him -- at the impressive age of 72 and growing younger by the year. Former colleagues were astonished, not only because of Herman's call at such an advanced age, but even more by this generally conservative congregation calling not one but two "social-action radicals" (colleagues in the denominational agency most under fire) to be its ministers. Yet it worked.

There followed a happy collegial ministry, with such a memorable preaching, teaching and pastoral ministry by Herman that the congregation took him to its heart. The church printed his sermons and prayers, begged him for talks on tough topics and generally lionized him. He helped to start a lively dinner and discussion group and counseled countless church members in crisis.

Herman helped to establish well-attended Second Hour Seminars for talk-back after worship and for serious discussions on controversial topics. He welcomed thoughtful disagreement and received criticism as a gift to be prized and considered carefully. He did insist that opponents try to relate their views on political and economic issues, as he tried to relate his own, to insights of the Bible they held in common.

So much did this congregation -- many of them staunch conservatives in politics -- take this "old liberal" to its heart that Herman grumbled and worried about his easy reception. He recalled that Jesus warned, "Beware when all men speak well of you." "I used to be known as a *dangerous radical*," Herman wrote, "but I fear they think of me now as merely, well, benign. At my age, they think I'm harmless. We shall have to do something about that."

When I was called to a church in New Britain, Reissig stayed on to lead the church in Old Greenwich. When the Reverend Paul Yinger was finally called as senior pastor, Herman resigned to facilitate a new leadership staff but remained a church member. The congregation promptly named him Pastor Emeritus, keeping him listed on the church staff and expecting him to preach and teach periodically. Herman responded with the seemingly immodest comment: "The award is most appropriate." After a pause he added: "I'll tell you why. Remember your Latin? *Emeritus* comes from the Latin: *E* means out; *Meritus* means he deserved it."

In his emeritus years, Herman agonized over the absence of organized reflection by the congregation on what kind of "yeast" this People of God are called to be in the world's loaf. He gave perhaps a dozen sermons and Second Hour talks on the marks of a faithful and effective church. Discussions of these stimulated many to re-think their assumptions about "proper" church life.

One little-noticed Reissig ministry developed in his correspondence, especially with conservative critics who wrote him of their discontent with some of his liberal utterances. Their discontent might be political, economic or theological. Herman took their letters very seriously and wrote such warm, detailed letters in return, free of all invective and polarization, that lives were changed -- by mail! A published volume of such exchanges, perhaps entitled " Liberal Letters to Conservative Christians," has even been proposed.

Of this unusual correspondence with members of the church, Herman wrote in 1982:

> I spend much of my time writing personal letters. If a Sunday congregation at First Church should be asked how many have had letters from me, hands would go up all over the place. This is partly the consequence of not mingling with people on most days. (Editor: His growing hearing loss embarrassed and handicapped him.) But I always wrote many letters, even in my most active years. . . The writer, Anatole Broyard, says of the writing of the French author, Roland Barthes: "Barthes prodded, squeezed, sniffed at language, like a great chef buying fruits and vegetables." That beautifully expresses my ideal in writing.

Reading, Writing and Ruminations

For more than 30 years during summer vacations and warm-weather weekends, Herman "got away from it all" with his wife to a little cabin in the woods of Gilead, Connecticut. Herman built this with his own hands. Little by little, over the years the cabin became a rough-hewn but comfortable oasis. It had built-in bunks, a rainwater barrel and a Franklin stove. There were surprising signs about the place, such as The Lydia Pinkham Room, The John F. Kennedy Promontory and The Richard Milhous Nixon Memorial Garden -- long before Watergate and only four feet square. For Herman there was truly "a balm in Gilead."

After retirement at 66 from his work as International Relations Secretary, Herman's reading took an intense theological turn. One year he reported to friends his most exciting reading for the past 12 months. He had read voraciously books by Roman Catholic theologians, especially some whose rebellion from Rome he admired. Two of these were *On Being a Christian* by Hans Kung and *A Theology of Liberation* by Gustavo Gutierrez.

Above all, it was Schillebeeckx's *Jesus: An Experiment in Christology*, which most profoundly affected him. He promptly declared it the most revelatory book on Jesus he had read in his entire life: When "I reached the last page of this massive study," he wrote, "do you know what I did? I started at page one and read it straight through again!. . . His vast erudition makes Bible stories come alive, mixed with cool reason and profound reverence. If I should ever meet this man I would astonish, and perhaps offend, him by throwing my arms around him."

He had read with excitement Tom Driver's *Synonyms for God*, argued with Watson, Coker and Clark's *Commitment Without Ideology*. Langdon Gilkey had especially impressed him, as in *Message and Essence*; *Taming the Whirlwind*; *The Renewal of God-Language*; *Shantung Compound*; and *How Can the Church Minister to the World Without Losing Itself*? Gilkey's writings (particularly *Taming*) encouraged Reissig in his own quest for fresher, unspoiled language for the divine dimension.

He had pondered John Cobb's *Process Theology* and Robert McAfee Brown's *Theology in a New Key* -- both for him new departures in theological method. He loved his old friend John

Bennett's *The Radical Imperative* ("great Christian teacher"). He was moved by *Autobiographies of Ten Religious Leaders* by Radoslav A. Tsanoff, especially the lives of Augustine, Bunyan, Renan, Tolstoy, Schweitzer and Pope John XXIII.

Herman had kept up to date in science with books like Bronowski's *The Ascent of Man* and Carl Sagan's *Broca's Brain*. After reading Peter Medawar's *Advice to a Young Scientist*, he corresponded with the Nobel Prize-winning author. "He is, to my mind," Herman wrote later, "an example of non-believing humanism at its best." A favorite to re-read was Loren Eisely's *The Star Thrower* ("instructs the mind and lifts the spirit"). He re-read pioneering early books on cosmology by Sir James Jeans and Arthur Eddington: "They killed the notion of a mechanistic universe."

All these, given for illustration, and many more were apparently read in only one typical year -- when the man was already over 80! This voracious reading and openness to new insights helps to explain Herman's remarkable intellectual skills and the creativity of his preaching and teaching to the end.

At age 85, Herman commented: "My ears are age 98, my eyes are age 75, but I can keep my spirit at age 30." Earlier, he had written in the Lakeland *Ledger* that he rebelled against becoming "gracefully irrelevant -- Life is too interesting to stand on the sidelines -- It's an old saying that the difference between a rut and a grave is only a question of depth." Herman read a claim of biologists and psychologists that if all through life we vigorously use our heads, we help to avoid old age senility. He promptly scribbled this couplet and presented it to his cardiologist:

If you keep on exercising your noodle
You can stay as spry as an Irish poodle.

On his 80th birthday, he was surprised ("bowled over," he said) by friends in the church with a "This Is Your Life" party.

His colorful iconoclasm in a grey world of dull respectability was celebrated in a song about his post-retirement career. One stanza:

Since then he has caused a sensation,
As preacher and prophet and friend.
Unpopular truth's his vocation
And helping all prigs to unbend.

At Herman Reissig's memorial service five years later, a remark of the jurist Oliver Wendell Holmes was remembered. Said Holmes in 1884, "I think that, as life is action and passion, it is required of a man that he should share the passion and action of his time, at peril of not to have lived."

That catches eloquently one side of Herman, sharing the social action and passion of his time. He had a lyrical side also, a side that savored and gulped and enjoyed life hugely, whether friends or food, the beauty of a woman, the grain of a block of wood, or the lowest notes of the 16-foot bourdon stop of the organ: he thrilled to feel the music "in his bones."

He wrote a paraphrase of the well-known hymn, "For all the saints," in appreciation of contemporary faith and courage. His began: "For living saints..." Herman's own prayers often expressed this appreciation of life in the moment. During a prayer on Music Sunday in First Church, Old Greenwich, Herman addressed himself in a paraphrase of Psalm 150:

Sing, my soul! Sing the greatness and wonder of life.
Sing faith against despair. Sing beauty against drabness.
Sing life against death.
With lifted voice, with string and horn,
with bell and organ pipe, with drum and cymbal,
sing the glory of God and the goodness of life.
O my soul, cease from sighing. Listen to the singing.

Herman Reissig listened to the singing until he himself became part of the Song. It is our hope that this sampling of his own lyrics will help to keep him singing to God, to the Church and to the world. With all three of these he remained all his life uneasily in love.

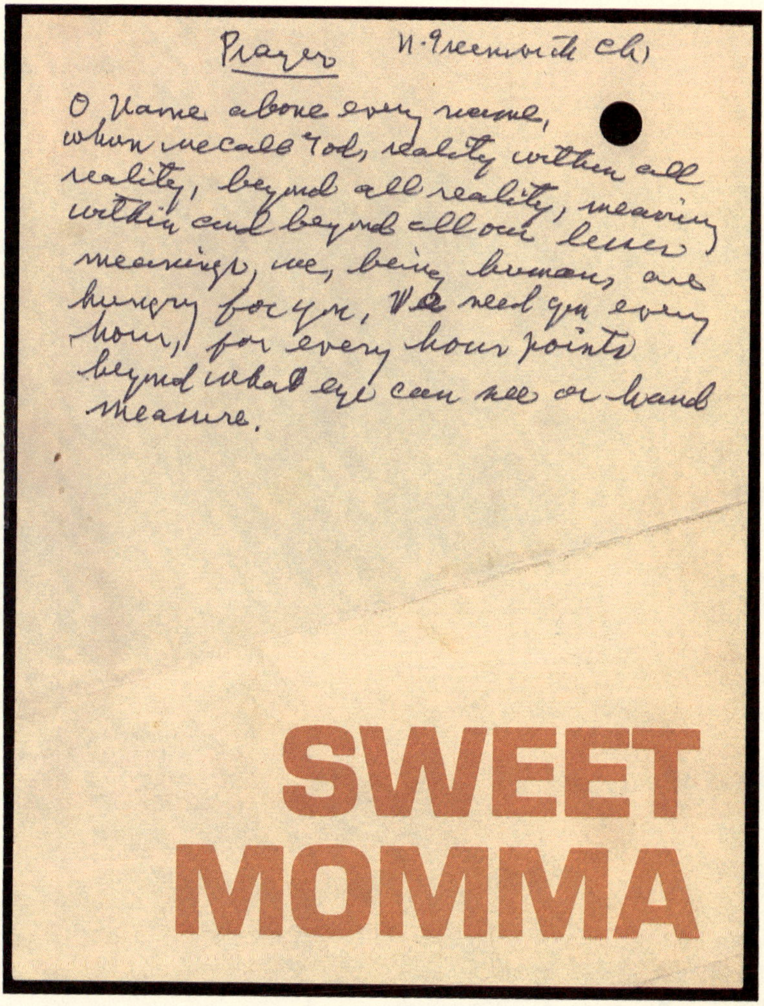

Prayer N. Greenwich Ch.

O Name above every name, whom we call God, reality within all reality, beyond all reality, meaning within and beyond all our lesser meanings, we, being human, are hungry for you, We need you every hour, for every hour points beyond what eye can see or hand measure.

SWEET MOMMA

When words of inspiration came to Herman, he did not let them escape.

Martha B. Porter, photographer

"If we are to have a living faith, we cannot go on speaking about God in ways that fit an older world but do not fit our world."

Chapter II. THE CHALLENGE IN PREACHING

By the Rev. Dr. Herman F. Reissig
(Written April, 1984,
as an introduction to a proposed book of his sermons.)

To a longtime friend, a highly competent pastor-preacher, I put a question. "Do you think we need a new religion?" His answer: "You may as well ask if we need a new law of gravitation." The answer came quickly. Too quickly.

Why would I ask such a question? And why did I think his answer unsatisfactory? One's religion may be defined as that center of personal beliefs from which one looks upon life in both its individual and social aspects, sometimes saying *Yes* to what one sees and sometimes *No*, sometimes a qualified *Yes* and sometimes a qualified *No*. In other words, to have a religion means to have a controlling center. To be a Christian means that this center from which one judges and acts is Jesus of Nazareth, called the Christ. To make "Christ" a part of his original name, saying "Jesus Christ," signifies that for Christians he was a fully human being and at the same time the local and authentic representative of God.

Today, western people live in a secularized world. What does that mean? It means that for most of us our center is not Jesus Christ, but the principles and ways of the prevailing culture. This is obviously the case with atheists, agnostics and with those who dismiss the Christian faith as superstition or as somcthing appropriate to the childhood of the race but which intelligent people are now outgrowing.

A closer look says that the transfer of the center from Christ to what is believed and practiced by the surrounding culture has also happened to Christians. Not to all but to many and perhaps to most. A simple test proves this to be the situation. Converse with church members, face to face or by letter. (I have for some years corresponded regularly with a number of active church members.)

Introduce almost any controversial question, from relations between the sexes to domestic economic or political issues to international affairs. The reasoning one hears is almost never based specifically on "the will of God." In the church they sing, "In the Cross of Christ I Glory," but outside the church they do not ask "What does the cross of Christ say about this issue?" When they object to a policy or way of thinking they say it isn't rational or it isn't intelligent or it is un-American or anti-capitalist or Marxist. A friend sent me several pages of comment on a book of sermons and lectures by a famous theologian. He had some objections. But he did not once write that the objectionable statements are contrary to the Christian faith; he wrote they are "biased." Biased against what? How do church members decide how to vote, what economic or political policies to support? What is it that makes a certain idea or practice desirable or wrong?

This is not to say that if we do not consciously and specifically refer to Christ and his teaching our opinions will be wrong. Still, will anyone claim that in the United States, to take only this one country, our society is so close to being Christian that it no longer needs Christian criticism? Has the kingdom of God, for whose coming Christians pray every Sunday, been so fully embodied in our society that Christians need no longer feel much tension between that kingdom and the way we live and conduct national affairs?

I am not thinking of people who are blatantly selfish and irresponsible: thieves, murderers, hard drug sellers, gamblers, pornographers. I am thinking of people who mean to be conscientious citizens, people who go to church. I am saying that the culture in which they live -- its prevailing political and economic ideas, its rational and scientific views -- has invaded their inner lives, so that the faith and the way of Christ have become blurred, and to choose Christ has lost any distinctive meaning.

Does it not look as if the Christian faith has lost its power to change and shape our living? Those who take their faith with real seriousness may feel they are like the children who, as pictured by Jesus, complain, "We piped to you but you did not dance."

(*Matthew 11:17*) So: Do we perhaps need a new religion, some new revelation and message that will pull us out of our darkness and drift and set our feet on the road to a more truly human existence? Has Christianity, for all the good it has done and still does, lost its vital power?

The sermons I have written are the wrestling of one minister of the Gospel with these questions. There have been hours when I was almost ready to give up. Considering my own personal resistance to allowing the faith and the way of Christ to control me, and seeing how our whole culture seems to go its own way with some praising Christ in church but paying little attention to him in everyday matters, I have ruminated on the question he has put to me.

In the past few years no one has helped me more to hang on to Christ than the great Dutch Catholic biblical scholar and theologian, Edward Shillebeeckx. His massive study, *Jesus, An Experiment in Christology*, was my spiritual food every morning for many weeks. His book, *God Among Us: The Gospel Proclaimed*, has helped to give me a living center for my own life. When one reads the Bible with this devout scholar the Bible speaks. Deeply sure of God, Schillebeeckx wears no blinders that hide either the weaknesses of today's churches or the facts of our culture. He is a *committed and liberated* Christian. He comes close to being what, it seems to me, every Christian should be today -- deeply committed to Christ while liberated both from traditional theological concepts or older views of the Bible and from conventional acquiescence in the ways of today's cultures.

One thing has for many years been clear to me: If we are to have a living faith, we cannot go on speaking about God in ways that fit an older world but do not fit our world. Nor can we interpret the humanity and the deity of Jesus in ways that were meaningful in the first or sixteenth centuries but that for modern people are only flat, objective statements without the feel of something immediate and personal. We are, one hopes, in these last years of the twentieth century, on the threshold of a new reformation, less dramatic and violent than the Reformation of the 16th century, but perhaps even more profound. No leaders stand out as much as Luther and Calvin stood out then. But the number of serious and luminous Christian minds increases. To some extent the new reformation will come from within the western world; to a perhaps larger degree it will come, as Harvey Cox believes, from the "base communities" of the Third World, especially those in Latin America. As the northern and western part of our globe is beginning to lose its dominating place in the political area, so those who have seemed marginal (to us) are becoming our teachers. This swing away from the northern, industrialized, technological societies can be observed in two prominent places -- in the United Nations and in the World Council of Churches. In the U.N. the loss of dominance by Europe and North America has created for the present, a somewhat chaotic and, to the northern nations, disillusioning situation. In the World Council of Churches it has produced statements and actions that seem very strange, if not downright wrong, to Christians in Europe and the United States. To interpret changes in these ecumenical organizations as due to the baleful influence of Marxism is superficial.

In recent years, I have been an occasional preacher, mainly to the First Congregational Church (United Church of Christ) in Old Greenwich, Connecticut. This church is perhaps not typical. Most of its people can be called affluent, most are college or university graduates, many are corporation executives or corporation lawyers, most would describe their social views as conservative. I came to the church in 1972 as an interim pastor, and have remained to preach intermittently to the year 1984. I was introduced to the church by a colleague as "a life-long liberal." I have learned much from the people of this church. What I may have contributed to them is for them to say. I know only that there has been a wonderfully warm personal relationship. The experience of these eleven years has taught me something about the possibility of mixing the prophetic and the pastoral ministries.

I shall add a comment that may be of some interest to those who have listened to my sermons. The comment is highly personal, but it may help to indicate how a "liberal" preacher can speak to, mainly, conservative folk without provoking discord. Throughout my ministry it has been my habit to write sermons with actual persons sitting on the other side of my desk. The subject has been chosen and the text selected, when there is one. How now to preach on this subject so that I will not be reading an essay addressed to the world in general, but will really be communicating to Mr. . . . and Mrs. . . . and Miss . . . sitting there in the pews? I hold their faces before me, recall what I know about them, try to put myself in their places. Will these words, this sentence, this analysis be real to them? This makes sermon preparation slow going. It means much meditation, much struggle with words. And this has meant secluding myself during most of the morning hours, alone with "the Word" and with the people to whom I speak. (Time enough in the afternoons and evenings for pastoral work and personal meetings.)

Is this more than the average pastor can manage? Preaching may not seem as important in the future as it has been in the past. There may well be more emphasis on group discussions and less on homiletic monologues. But I maintain that as long as we expect people to listen for twenty or more minutes to a sermon, the pastor-preacher (the two should never be separated) is under the most solemn obligation to set aside many hours -- uninterrupted and preferably in the morning when the mind is fresh -- for sermon preparation. It might just be that if more pastor-preachers did this, our Sunday services of worship might be real *events*, less dull or less dependent for their appeal on what I have called "slightly baptized entertainment."

Helen S. Allen, artist

"A good church will resist any tendency to isolate itself from the whole Christian church and will have a lively awareness of being a part of the tissue of a world-wide Christian movement."

Chapter III. THE CHURCH

Edited by Mary Lou Woods, Ruth and Richard Pope, parishioners,
First Congregational Church of Greenwich,
Old Greenwich, Connecticut

Herman Reissig spent his life examining and re-examining central concepts such as "The Church." He wrote about them to friends in his many letters; he talked about them; he preached them -- but he was never finished with them. They were looked at from many angles, from history, and again from that of modern practices, and still another time from the ideas of great thinkers. He polished off this view one time, added a new concept the next, re-defined another idea the next time. He was impatient with people limiting great concepts by their own needs or imperfections, but he kept trying to help us see the role of the Church in revealing and nourishing great religious ideas.

Church Growth

In letters, Herman expressed some thoughts on church growth:

> Suppose we take the assertion, "God is Love" and instead of thinking of all objections to this belief, in our own personal lives and in the history of human beings, we should ask what this assertion means for our conduct as persons and as church members. A church -- large, middle or small -- that actually reaches out in love, past all barriers of status, race, nationality, geography, might have no difficulty in winning new members. But the love would have to be active and limitless, a vigorous reaching out to people. A question about "church growth": Does concentration on church growth tend to concentrate the church on itself? As if the purpose of the Christian faith were large and thriving churches! Suppose we

forgot about church growth and thought only about human growth: the opportunity for everyone to develop in mind and body. The church that loses its life shall save it and the church that saves its life shall lose it.

The more I think about this, the more sure I am that you have to be careful in talking about and urging church growth. Jesus did not live and die for church growth. His purpose was human growth, human liberation, human prosperity. Let the church get its mind off itself and on men, women and children! The institutional church is a means, not an end.

(Letter, April 21, 1983)

Evangelism is not primarily reaching out for new church members. It begins with a vital personal faith that people wish to share. And, personal faith will not become alive in people today unless we speak of God and of Christ in ways that fit what we know about our world and about human beings.

We have some creative theological thinkers in the seminaries but mighty few in the denominational bureaucracies. Our bureaucrats are too busy with institutional problems.

Therefore: He best helps churches to grow who best helps persons to find a living faith. An inner and spiritual urge will be creative in the practical level -- putting a greeter at the door, etc. (Letter, April 30, 1983)

Going to Church

Herman had requested letters from the congregation about what coming to church meant to them. In his sermon "What's the Use of Going to Church?", he responded to some of the letters:

A man who wrote that he goes to church to look at himself "from the inside," ends by saying, "Going to church makes me feel humble again." If going to church does not sometimes make you feel humble -- sometimes more than humble, downright wretched about the poor use we make of life -- then there is something wrong, either with you or with the worship and the preaching. That is why we ministers wish the dear people who tell us at the door they "enjoyed" the service would find a better way of saying it. Some day I would love to hear some worshipper say, "I did not enjoy it one bit, but I'm sure it was good for me."

In the latter part of this sermon, he made personal witness, as was his wont:

> And now in a few sentences, I shall say what going to church means to me. In addition to the fellowship, the sense of belonging, the feeling of something beyond eating and drinking and earning a living, in addition to joy in the beauty of this Meeting House, the great music, the pleasure of the smile and the handclasp, beyond all those good things going to church means to me having a dialogue with the man Jesus of Nazareth, what He was, what He taught, and with God whom He set before us, a God who comforts, yes, who makes me flinch, who makes my conscience uncomfortable, the God who will not let me rest where I am and where my world is, the God of the whole of life -- family, sex relations, sports, politics, economic life, government, international relations, everything important to human beings. This for me is a place for dialogue with the man Jesus who showed us what it is to be truly human, and with a God who is both immanent and infinitely transcendent.
>
> (Sermon, August 31, 1980)

Christ's Church

A sermon, "Where is the Church?", was a fine example of the depth and breadth of Herman Reissig's scholarship. During a long discussion of the historical concept of "church," he subtly challenged the congregation. The problems are, as usual, universal ones and we are all involved in and responsible for their solutions. He concludes:

> Let us now set a view of the church that to increasing numbers of Christians seems more faithful to Christ and also truer to what we can see as we look around in our world. The traditional idea was: Christ is where the church is. To see

Christ at work, to observe his spirit, you looked at the church. To serve Christ you joined a church and worked in and through it. The other idea is: The church of Christ is wherever Christ is. Between these two conceptions lies a profound difference. The old view had the effect of confining Christ, making him a possession of the church. No church, no Christ. . .

But if we say, not Christ is where the church is, but the true church is wherever Christ is, then we have a wider, deeper and truer conception of the church, and for some of us a much more inspiring conception.

Where do you think Christ is in our contemporary world? On the basis of what we can know about him from the New Testament we must, I think, say at least the following:

- Wherever children are received with love, given, as they grow, wise and loving care, are encouraged to do justly, to love mercy and to walk humbly before God, there Christ is present and there he is at work, whether the organized church is there or not.
- Where the minds of people, young and old, are given knowledge, trained to think, made receptive to all the riches of life, there Christ is present and there the true church can be found.
- Where the sick are healed, cared for with sympathy and competence by doctors, nurses, relatives, friends, there is Christ and there is his church.
- Where the emotionally disturbed, the mentally retarded, the crippled, blind, deaf are given the assistance they need, there is the living Christ and there is his true church.
- Where old people in their loneliness and frailty are given companionship and patient help, there Christ may be found and there is Christ's church.
- Where men and women struggle against injustice, anywhere in the world; where those who are strong help to bear the burdens of those who are weak; where people look beyond their own safety and comfort and show they care for their

neighbors, there Christ walks, and there walks with him his real church.

- Wherever human beings, faced by moral choice, struggle to choose what is good and true; wherever they turn from what is hurtful to what is helpful; wherever they help to liberate and unite; wherever hostility is replaced by reconciliation, there Christ is alive and there is the body of Christ.
- Where men and women yearn and work for peace, for good government, for cities that are healthy and humane; where they seek to make farm, factory, office an instrument not only for profit but for human well-being, there Christ may be discerned and there is his church.

All this means that if we look to see where Christ is alive in our world we may find him in surprising places. It means that the church is not an institution apart from the common life. It means that the true church of Christ is a large umbrella, under which are gathered many kinds of people, many agencies and institutions, some of which are not called "church."

(Sermon, May 1, 1972)

Characteristics of a Good Church

Herman preached four sermons on the "Characteristics of a Good Church." In the second of these, he expressed concern about our preoccupation with our own little lives and community:

A good church will resist any tendency to isolate itself from the whole Christian church and will have a lively awareness of being a part of the tissue of a worldwide Christian movement.

I have never been what we call a "denominationalist," that is one who thinks his own denomination is superior to all others. I like the United Church of Christ, which in its polity is essentially Congregational, but I could live as a Christian and preach the Gospel in a Methodist or Presbyterian or Baptist or Lutheran or Episcopal church and even, if the Pope would loosen up a little on some matters, in a Catholic church. Sectarianism is not to my taste.

But worse even than being a denominational sectarian is to be a local church provincial, as if one local church were self-sufficient and need not pay attention to the church that exists beyond its walls. I plead this morning for a truly inclusive ecumenical church.

There are two main ways in which we may discover if the God we know through Jesus Christ is relevant to our human problems: the way of thinking, that is, the way of theology, and the way of action. The two ways belong together. Right actions depend on good thinking, but theology apart from Christian action is a mere verbalism.

The business of finding a theology that speaks to us today where we actually live certainly cannot be conducted on a merely local level. We need help from many Christians in many places and in many situations, from Christians in Latin America, in Asia and Africa. And here lies a fundamental value to us of the National Council of Churches and the World Council of Churches. In these ecumenical agencies, constant, probing thinking is going on; thinking about the Bible and what it has to say to us, thinking about how today we can picture God, thinking about the meaning of Christ. The present banner-word of the World Council of Churches is "Jesus Christ is Lord." Is He? In what way? You will not read about this activity of the World Council of Churches in business magazines, valuable as they may be. Nevertheless, Jesus Christ and His meaning for us is *the* central concern of the World Council. . .

All the finest thinking and writing and verbalizing in the world will not convince our godless generation that the God of Christ matters unless Christian actions are in accord with Christian beliefs.

(Sermon, September 12, 1982)

In a Second Hour following the church service, Herman made this statement in examining the purpose and character of a church:

The worth of our church is not to be measured by the number of members. A large church can be less *worthful* than a small church. Our church is not to be measured by the quality of its physical building. A little group of persons meeting in a simple frame structure with a leaking roof could be more meaningful than a thousand persons assembled in a cathedral. A church is not to be measured by counting the number of people who come to the church on Sundays and weekdays. Such statistics are interesting but not finally significant. A church is not to be measured by the quality of its music or the eloquence of its preaching. The justly admired Quakers have neither music nor sermons. Finally, in this series of negatives, the name "First Congregational Church" tells us nothing about our worth. The word "Congregational" denotes merely a form of organization, and the word "First" says only that this church was here in chronological advance of any other church.

(Second Hour, September 23, 1984)

The World Church

He kept reminding us of the importance of the World Council of Churches, of the contributions of seminaries and the strength of ecumenical ties; we cannot be self-sufficient. This is an excerpt from his sermon "Characteristics of the United Church of Christ":

While there is some pride in historical background, the UCC is not so much tradition-minded or denomination-minded as, in aim, Christ-minded. It is centrally a "free" church, not bound by historic creeds or by a literal reading of an "infallible" Bible, and not determined from above in hierarchical fashion. Leadership: *Yes*. Domination: *No*.

It is a pluralistic church, and aims to be as pluralistic as humanity: white, black, brown, European, Asian, Hispanic, native American Indian.

It is a United and *uniting* church, deeply ecumenical, seeking constantly to overcome historic and no longer meaningful divisions of the church of Christ on earth, a church that reaches out, rejects isolationism and provincialism.

> It pays attention to social relations and social institutions because it cares about the individual person, recognizing no line between personal religion and social religion. There is, therefore, strong emphasis on the most urgent issues of our times, education, sexual relations. There is, in short, constant concern with the total culture. It encourages all people, ordained and lay, to analyze political and economic and general cultural ideas and practices in the light of the mind of Christ.
>
> (Sermon, November 28, 1983)

Herman gave some specific examples about involvement of the world church in a presentation "Church Leaders and the World of Business" at a Second Hour following the church service:

> 1920 was the year of the great steel strike which went on and on and caused much personal suffering and economic dislocation. At that time steel mill workers were on a two-shift basis, twelve hours each. The workers asked for an eight-hour day; management said the eight-hour day would ruin the steel industry. The Federal Council of Churches, predecessor of the National Council of Churches, set up a high-level commission to investigate; the commission said the workers were right and management wrong. For this, the Federal Council suffered heavy criticism. After a few years, no steelman wanted to go back to the twelve-hour day.
>
> Ten years before President Nixon opened the door to China, a National Conference on World Order organized by the National Council of Churches said that the exclusion of mainland China from the community of nations made no sense. In my own travels among the churches, I had to deal with many denunciations of the National Council for being "soft on communism," or worse. The fault of the National Council's study conference seems to have been that it was right a little before some people considered it time to be right. The Christian church is not supposed to echo public opinion. It should be at least a little ahead of the times, or at odds with public opinion.
>
> (Second Hour, January 22, 1984)

Being Responsible -- Stewardship

Herman recognized the value of a dollar, and was careful with his money; but he led by example in his generosity to the church:

> The sermon topic will, I think, be "On Being a Responsible Person." One result of the sermon and its preparation will be that the preacher will have to increase his pledge or else detect a hollow ring in his own words to the congregation. Next Monday I am, on my suggestion, to meet with the trustees and I shall ask them to let me know in advance of the sermon on stewardship the aggregate by which they, the trustees, intend to increase their pledges, my intention being to announce this to the congregation near the end of the sermon. If the trustees should decline to do this I am inclined to say, "Well, then, I won't preach." Those few to whom I have communicated what I will ask of the trustees think it is a "splendid" idea.
>
> (Letter, July 18, 1975)

He concluded one of his finest sermons, "Characteristics of a Good Church III," with this paragraph:

> This is stewardship month in our church. How do we decide how much to give to the church and to other helping agencies? It could be helpful to aim at ten percent, just so we don't think tithing is going to win special favors from God. I think we should decide how much to give on the basis of a simple fact: You and I owe something; we owe a lot. We would not have a red cent without the help of others and of our whole society. And why should anyone put money into the treasury of this church? Is it not for the purpose of making the First Congregational Church conspicuous for goodness and compassion?
>
> (Sermon, October 10, 1982)

(The full text of this sermon can be found in Appendix I.)

Christian Leadership

Herman was a prolific letter writer. Of course, we expect that to happen with long-distance friends, but the letter below is to a parishioner he saw in person on a regular basis. Corresponding gave him the opportunity to develop his thinking:

> If we ask about the main requirements in good Christian leadership, no line should be drawn between good motives, sincerity, and personal integrity, on the one hand, and superior intellectual ability, on the other. The leaders I have known and admired, or read about, have had both. If we had to choose between the two, I am sure most of us would prefer just plain "goodness."
>
> In my own experience, it has been my good fortune to have had some association with some of the strongest minds in the churches: George Buttrick, Henry Sloane Coffin, Harry Emerson Fosdick, Reinhold Niebuhr, Ralph Sockman, Paul Scherer, Bishop Oxnam, John C. Bennett - - to name only those who come instantly to mind.
>
> All of these had exemplary character and a strong pastoral instinct. To single out just one of them, George Buttrick commanded attention for his pulpit work and was also a real scholar, but no one ever said he was not a thoughtful pastor. Harry Fosdick was the most brilliant preacher of his time, but Fosdick gave every afternoon to consultation with individuals who needed counseling. Knowing history and having penetrating minds did not prevent these men from being congenial, thoughtful friends. They were a delight to know on the personal level and their preaching was something one did not soon forget. If we go back over the history of the Christian church we have to say, I think, that those leaders who powerfully influenced the Christian movement and individual Christians were almost always great intellects. Here are a few of them:
>
> *St. Paul* - by far the most powerful thinker in the early church
>
> *St. Augustine* - who is still read and studied
>
> *Martin Luther* - who knew enough Hebrew and Greek to translate the whole Bible

John Wesley - who was not perhaps a great scholar, but was a man of eminently superior ability

Albert Schweitzer - who on one side was a simple, humble missionary to Africa, but also recognized as a great scholar.

These men and scores of others who might be cited set the Christian enterprise forward. They were great teachers, truly learned men. All this is not to say that every pastor should be a genius. I believe, however, that one of the reasons for declining church membership lies here: the overwhelming majority of the men and women who are spiritual leaders of our churches are hard- working, sincere, trustworthy, but for various reasons they do not command wide respect in showing how the ancient faith can be made vital in our changing and troubled time. There are today too many conscientious and intelligent persons who are not in our churches and I think this is due, in large part, to weakness in the teaching-preaching ministry. There is in our churches too much reliance on such things as music and sociability. These things are important and valuable, but they do not compensate for serious dealing with the fundamentals of religion.

It is disconcerting to meet with a group of church members (as I did recently on four Wednesday evenings) and to see how weak a grasp they have on what the Bible says and on how to read it, on how we can today think of God, on the meaning of Christ.

There can, I think, be no strong Christianity without hard and careful thinking. Most of our pastors are too busy with general pastoral work and with administration of the church to leave time for the kind of teaching-preaching leadership I have in mind. I am certainly not suggesting that the pulpit be turned into a place for intellectual discourses or that we should expect all our people to be "intellectuals."

But if ministers should appeal to the heart, they should also nourish and challenge the mind.

(Letter, undated)

Herman suggested a possible solution to the problem of Christian leadership in his Second Hour comments on "Church Leaders and the World of Business":

> There has been and still is some truth in the belief that business people are children in the general field of culture: art, music, literature, history, sociology, psychology, theology; and there has been, and still is, some truth in the perception of ministers as rank amateurs in the business and political worlds. Many business persons never argue a position on a public issue from a stand on the Bible or Christian theology because, as they freely admit, they don't feel at home in those areas. Many ministers stay clear of concrete illustration of religious truths taken from business and politics because either they distrust their own competence, or they are afraid of stepping on the toes of business people or politicians. A local church may then be kept in happy unity by praise of lofty abstractions on which everyone can agree, and by giving money and direct personal service to charitable causes, which is indeed helpful, but does not disturb basic political and economic beliefs and practices. In communist countries, church leaders are forbidden to talk about politics on pain of imprisonment or worse. In capitalist countries, church leaders are warned against taking positions on political and economic issues on threat of having their income cut off.
>
> Both situations seem to me highly unsatisfactory and dangerous, both to the common good and to the integrity of the Christian enterprise. What is to be done? In very general terms, this unsatisfactory situation can be ameliorated, though never completely cured, by having business people better educated in the Bible, theology and Christian history, and having ministers broaden their education to include more political science, economics, and secular history. Beyond this prescription, there is here and there arising the opinion that the distinction between ordained and lay Christians should be abolished. I am inclined to think there is something in the idea. A suggestion on how this would work is in

the Worker-Priest experiment, which was strong in France a few decades ago and which is still alive.

(Second Hour, January 22, 1984)

Diversity in the Church

Uneasiness about supporting an organization, including the church, when one has personal objections, is discussed in this letter:

It can probably be said that every large organization does some things with contributed money to which some contributors object. For example, I have the uneasy feeling that a part of the money I pay for gasoline is used by oil companies for general political propaganda purposes with which I am not in sympathy. About this I can do nothing, if I want to drive my car. Many church expenses are hidden under such general categories in the published budget that I cannot know in detail how my contribution is used. A church member has the right to know the details, but few would have the courage to stand up at an Annual Meeting and ask for details.

I shall not, despite some uneasiness, withhold my support of the church. There is no way of keeping one's self "pure" in our world. I shall not try to use dubious loopholes in paying income taxes because I do not like the present administration or because I am against the excessive amounts spent on armaments.

There is no way in which an organization supported by voluntary gifts can ask each individual giver for his/her consent. Nor can everybody be asked to express an opinion on resolutions and pronouncements by church bodies. Pure democracy is unworkable in any large organization of society. This means that, unless I want to play the hermit, I have to swallow hard about many things done by my country, my business organizations, my church. We can and should work toward a more participatory society, but no matter how many participate, none of us can always have his/her way. It could also be that my personal objections are not well-advised.

(Letter, January 17, 1982)

In a sermon, "Diversity Without Discord," Herman commented further on diversity, both outside and within the Church:

> The world would be poorer if everyone had the same religion. Christians, Jews, Buddhists, Hindus look at the stars through different telescopes and none has the whole truth. We sometimes wish the world had one common language, but a language grows out of long ethnic or national experience, and if all the world's people spoke English or French or Chinese we would lose something precious. Fascism and communism try to enforce uniformity, with unhappy and short-term success. Democracy thrives on tolerance of differences. This makes democracy a little awkward.
>
> A former American diplomat put it in a picture. A dictatorship, he said, is like a big ship: all beautifully fitted together, nothing out of place, smooth, efficient. But the ship strikes an iceberg and the whole thing goes to the bottom. A free society, he said, is like a raft: unsinkable, but, damn it, your feet are always wet.
>
> Egotistic and conceited as we often are, let's not dream of a world in which everyone thinks like we think. If a church member wants his church to die, there is a way to kill it: demand that all the members, including the minister, have the same ideas about worship, music, theology, church government, social action and all the rest.
>
> (Sermon, November 26, 1972)

In another sermon "Let's Be Controversial," Herman challenged the contemporary church:

> Jesus had a vision of what human life *could* be. So, loving people, how could he be silent about things that kept them on a low level? If harmony had to be bought at the price of keeping quiet about things that offended God and made life less than it could be, the price was too high.
>
> What should be our conclusion with respect to a contemporary church? To be sure, no preacher and no church

member is a duplicate of Jesus; that fact we would better not forget! Still, we are supposed to follow this man who was discomforting as well as comforting. Or, is anyone bold enough to claim that we today are entitled to be so pleased with ourselves that all we need is a big smile and a pat on the back? Must we not rather say something like this: any church that always leaves us feeling good, any church that buys peace at the price of staying with large generalities with which everyone can agree, is not doing its job as a church of Jesus Christ. In sum, let us not put too much emphasis on harmony; let us instead ask for truthfulness and moral seriousness.

We grow by listening to and debating with other persons who may see what we have not seen. Our individual ideas are clarified, expanded, sometimes changed. Especially in our time, a church should be a beehive of discussion. Your opponent may just possibly be a messenger of God leading you to fuller life. Let cows and sheep have their untroubled composure. We human beings have the pain and the tonic of controversy.

(Sermon, April 27, 1980)

Social Action

Herman felt strongly that the local church should play a vital role in Christian social action. In the last chapter of his book *Man's New Home*, he discussed "The Roots of Christian Social Action" and concluded with these paragraphs:

That part of the Christian mission we call social action is not to be equated with liberalism or conservatism, with socialism or capitalism, with any political party or social panacea. Its center of interest is not politics or an economic system or the nation or the social order. Its whole concern is with persons. And because it cares, first and last, about this man, this woman, this child -- whatever the race, class, creed, or nationality -- it summons us to act with and through all the relationships and institutions that form the environment within which the person exists.

> In brief, Christian social action is Christian love of the neighbor -- love that knows what a man is, serves him where he is, and is resolved that the social order and all its institutions shall contribute to his fulfillment.
>
> (*United Church Press*, 1964)

(The complete text of this chapter from *Man's New Home* can be found in Appendix II.)

In another section of his book, *Man's New Home*, Herman discussed man's denial of being sinful as the great obstacle to effective social action:

> In speaking of the human person we have said that he has, according to our faith, an infinite worth. But the same religion insists that man is a sinner. Next to the denial of man's worth, the denial that he is a sinful being has been the great obstacle to the successful handling of social problems. If we do not believe that every human being is infinitely worthful, we move logically toward such results as racism, Nazism (including genocide), or toward the worst manifestations of communism. If we say we believe in the worth of the individual person but do not keep this belief in the center of our thinking about social problems, we get slums, racial discrimination, and pursuit of power and wealth for their own sake, all of which are so prevalent in democratic "Christian" societies.
>
> (*United Church Press*, 1964)

(The complete text of this excerpt from *Man's New Home* can be found in Appendix II.)

Herman later defined Christian social action in a sermon "Personal Religion: An Interpretation of Christian Social Action:"

> We may now be ready for a definition of Christian social action. The definition can be short and simple. Christian social action is the effort to make laws, our public ways and customs, and our social institutions as friendly as possible to the well-being of persons. Personal well-being is in the

center -- not ideologies, nor party politics, not national prestige, not social customs, not financial profit, not anything but flesh and blood men, women and children. It is for them that we go to legislative assemblies to ask that a law be enacted or changed. It is for them that we discuss taxation, housing, race relations, criminal justice, international affairs.

(Sermon, April 6, 1975)

* * *

Herman Reissig treated the church like a favorite child not using its talents wisely or living up to its potential, so needing chiding from time to time.

The Church, in Herman's opinion, exists wherever people are acting Christ-like; it is not limited to a specific building with activities on a specific day or days. Its success is not measured in number of members but in the depth of commitment of each of its members. We need the local church, the national church, the ecumenical church to nourish our roots, he insisted. Yet we are continually in danger of losing sight of our strength and our purpose.

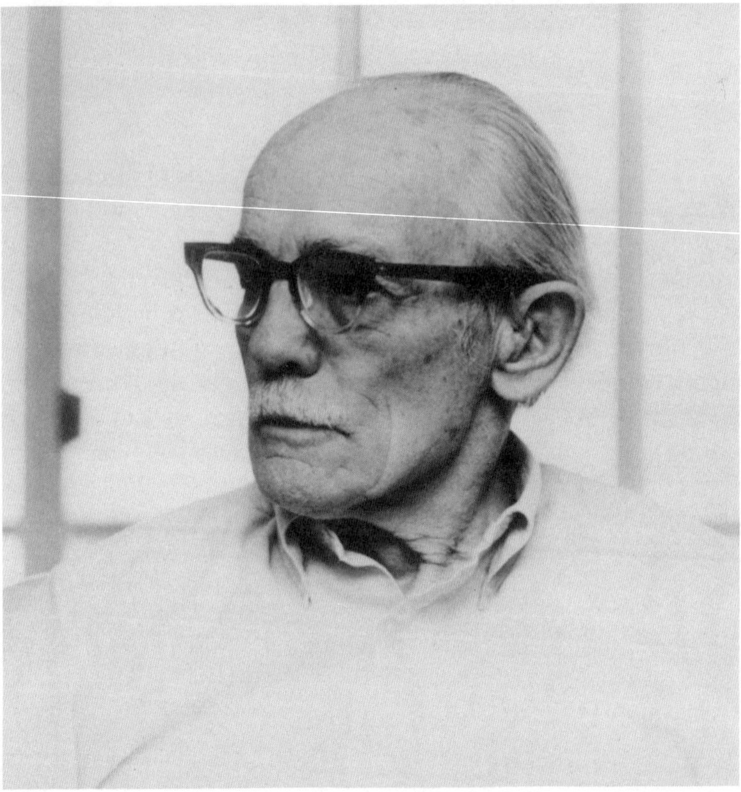

Martha B. Porter, photographer

"In anthem, hymn, scripture reading, prayer or sermon, you can hear words of courage and faith."

Chapter IV. WORSHIP

Edited by Richard Vogt, Director of Music,
First Congregational Church of Greenwich,
Old Greenwich, Connecticut

Herman Reissig may not have been a saint, but he looked and sounded like one. And in worship, through sermons, prayers and music, he reached down and lifted our hearts and minds to new levels of understanding and commitment. He fashioned services with care, weeks ahead of a particular Sunday. He worked at worship:

> Worship is a celebration of the wonder of life. Who, in the hour of worship, can feel cocky, proud or self- satisfied? As a hymn says, "My God, how wonderful thou art!" When we say "God" we must be filled with awe. We can be thankful, but we must also feel very humble. When we enter a place of worship our very breath should go deeper. The world and human life are big with marvels and wonders. O come, let us worship and bow down.
>
> (Sermon, June 24, 1979)

> Why do we worship? Not because God needs our praise, making him a monarch who loves praise. We worship a) because we need to judge all lesser gods by the greatest God, b) it is psychologically good to express admiration and gratitude, and c) we need to see ourselves in the light of the highest we know, and so repent.
>
> (Call to Worship, date unknown)

> Every day is a day the Lord has made. We are come together this day to learn again that all days are sacred, every hour a time for a new beginning, every life worthy of respect!

> Come, let us worship and bow down. Let us kneel before the Lord our maker.
>
> (Call to Worship, February 29, 1976)

Words and Music

Herman helped us to take hold of life. His words became mirrors that made us discover where we fell short. He nudged us, he prodded us, he shoved us along the rocky road of life:

> Living Christ, once long ago you joined us here on earth, sharing our life to the full; its happiness, its sorrow, even the death that waits for us all. But then you showed us how death is conquered by the power of the spirit. And still you walk with us on every road, sometimes in tender compassion, sometimes in stern admonition. It is your life on earth today and your still-living presence that brings us here today. And we believe you are the human face of God, so that we can carry any burden, overcome weakness, face death itself and not be afraid.
>
> (Pastoral Prayer, Easter Day, 1979)

I don't remember when I first met Herman Reissig, but what captured my attention in that first sermon I heard was his command of language. He was careful with words. He used them to paint vivid pictures. He tickled our ears as in these excerpts from his first sermon on "Characteristics of a Good Church":

> Let us spend a few minutes walking near the shore of our subject before we swim out to deep water.
>
> A man approached Jesus and asked, "What good thing must I do to gain eternal life?" Jesus said, "Why do you ask me about what is good? One is good." Goodness in human beings and in their institutions is always a highly relative quality. Before the ultimate Goodness, any claim to human goodness is an absurdity. Self-satisfaction in persons or in institutions is in fact the mortal enemy of goodness. The most we can claim for any church is that it is trying to be a better church.

Wife and husband don't do the dishes together anymore, talking as they work. The dishes are hastily rinsed, slipped into a machine, after which the couple goes to another room to sit in front of another machine that tells them to buy a machine-made adhesive that will keep their machine-made teeth from falling out when they eat machine-processed food.

One of the latest bits of what we call progress is the introduction to our schools of teaching machines. A human pupil will no longer sit with a human being called teacher but in front of a machine that shows numbers, statistics, facts, maps and maybe a bloodless figure saying something. Hospital nurses, God bless them, are hurried, sometimes harried. Who are you, lying there in the bed? You are "the patient in room twenty-six." We are commuters, customers, clients, numbers on a charge card, an item in the population census. The dehumanizing technology reaches its hideous climax in nuclear missiles that can be sent on their murderous errands at the push of a button.

Look, sister, brother! When you come here you are not a customer, a taxpayer, a commuter, a patient, a voter, an executive, a secretary, a homemaker, a provider, a lawyer, a teacher, a lay person, a pastor, a liberal, a conservative, a Republican, a Democrat. You are -- what? Basically -- and in church we are supposed to get down to basics -- basically, you are that stunning, bewildering, exhilarating, exasperating product of nature and of God we call a human being. That's enough.

(Sermon, May 16, 1982)

Despite gradual hearing loss, Herman had a great love and appreciation for music:

The effect of music cannot be expressed in prose, but I shall risk a few adjectives, nouns and verbs. Music speaks of the transcendent, of a world beyond the grubby, pedestrian terrain. Music speaks of harmony, beauty, glory. Whether it thunders or whispers, music takes us to where we think we ought to be. Music substitutes wings for plodding feet. Music

> wipes the dust from our spirits. John Ruskin said that Gothic cathedrals are "frozen music," which says something true about both great cathedrals and great music.
>
> (Lecture, February 23, 1984)

> When listening to a great concert or to our own organ and choir, who can believe we are the accidental result of mindless chemicals and electrical impulses?
>
> (Sermon, January 11, 1981)

Herman loved hymns, especially the power of the words involved. The tune was not all that important, and he could be convinced to pick a different tune if he could have his way with the words. He chose hymns he could use to build a service. He would ask for opinion (again, weeks ahead) and then write a note or call back with a comment, or debate choices and cancel out every one of them, for one reason or another. We had some lively discussions. He used hymns to capture the moment, as indicated in these further excerpts from his sermon "Characteristics of a Good Church":

> I want to talk about our difficulty in just one area, in the hymns we sing in the church. Many of our hymns were written in a world that is gone, just gone. But let me speak first of some hymns that do speak to us where we live. George Matheson went blind, a terrible loss for anyone, not the least for him as a minister. He had other troubles. Out of his darkness he wrote the hymn, "O Love that wilt not let me go, I rest my weary soul in thee." And mark the words of this blind man: "O Light, that followest all my way, I yield my flickering torch to thee." In many an hour, sometimes in bed at night, I have taken that hymn into my inner being. There is something here that, against all my intellectual, moral and spiritual difficulties, will not let me go.
>
> John Henry Newman was a clergyman in the Anglican Church. His faith evaporated. Before he found a new home in the Catholic Church, he wandered in painful darkness. In those days he wrote, "Lead, kindly light, amid the encircling

gloom, lead thou me on. The night is dark and I am far from home." That speaks powerfully to many a man and woman today.

Harry Emerson Fosdick was spending the summer on the coast of Maine. In the fall his new church, The Riverside Church, was to be dedicated. Have you seen that pile of architectural splendor, that glittering ecclesiastical palace?

Fosdick took his religion seriously, with passionate emotion. In Maine he thought about that building and that rich congregation, thought about the world swirling around it, yearned, prayed that The Riverside Church would be a true church of Christ, and so thinking, he wrote a hymn for the dedication service: "God of grace and God of glory, on thy people pour thy power... Cure thy children's warring madness, bend our pride to thy control."

(Sermon, May 16, 1982)

Herman continued with rage over some hymns and other liturgy and the imagery they set forth, particularly some of the old gospel hymns. *There Is a Fountain Filled With Blood?* Forget it! Not in his backyard!

A large number of the hymns we sing in church can be sung only with lungs, larynx and lips; mind and emotions cannot go along. Their imagery comes out of a dead world. So with scores of phrases and images in our hymns. The words are totally unreal or wrong or downright offensive.

(Sermon, May 16, 1982)

In a sermon "Atonement – What Did the Death of Christ Accomplish," he commented further about what is lacking in our liturgical worship:

My friends, it is our problem today that many of our hymns and much of the rest of our liturgical worship come out of a theology that no really thoughtful person accepts. We are today in the throes of a rethinking, a reformulation of our belief as Christians.

I, for one, would like to live long enough, though I shall not live that long, to worship with words that do not offend my mind. I do not require that I understand everything with my reason. Good heavens, no! I want a faith that leaps and sings, a faith with awe and beauty and power to command me. I do not want a religion of poetry and music. But the world of the first century or of the Middle Ages or of the 19th century is not my world. For our own sakes, for the sake of our grandchildren and for the sake of all the oncoming generations we must not mindlessly, lazily, continue to say, either in hymn or sermon, what we do not believe.

(Sermon, March 11, 1979)

When the imagery of a hymn text was no longer appropriate for today, Herman wrote his own text:

For Living Saints Who Labor Bravely On
Tune: Sine Nomine

For living saints who labor bravely on,
Who keep the faith through battles lost or won,
To Christ, their leader, let our praise be sung:
Alleluia! Alleluia!

In days of joy, in suffering's darkest night,
Be thou, O Christ, their constant, shining light,
That none may falter in the fiercest fight:
Alleluia! Alleluia!

O may all Christians be as true and bold
As those who lived and died in days of old,
That in our time the Good News may be told:
Alleluia! Alleluia!

Bind all together in love's service strong,
Fighting for all 'gainst ev'ry human wrong,
That all may join in resurrection song:
Alleluia! Alleluia!

Using the Pulpit

Herman Reissig expressed his thoughts on a preacher's responsibility:

> A good church will take seriously the old Protestant principle of the free pulpit. Surely it is a great error to suppose that the sermon should present all sides of a question. The preacher is under the most solemn obligation to study and think and pray and then to interpret questions of faith and ethics as he sees them, never, but never, trying to accommodate the sermon to majority opinion.
>
> Would you trust a physician who had the reputation of telling patients only what they want to hear? The honest physician can be mistaken, as every physician knows. So can the preacher, including this one. But kindness that does not include rigorous honesty is self-love in the preacher, not true love for others. Let a preacher, let a church make mistakes -- just so they do not deserve the poisonous adjective "bland."
>
> (Sermon, May 16, 1982)

Herman orchestrated worship. He chose blocks of sound, spoken and sung, to build a theme you would remember:

> The Lord is in his holy temple, which is the world of people and of nature. He speaks in the silence and also in the noisy street, in the place we call church and also in home, office and the truck driver's cab, in prayer meetings and also in legislative chambers. We are here in this place to learn how to hear his voice in every place.
>
> (Call to Worship, April 25, 1975)

Herman peppered me with memos, phone calls, suggestions for anthems, changes in the worship order -- would I sing a brief bit at the close of a sermon? "Please ask the choir to sing this little verse. I will turn around during the sermon and you can do it then." In simple words, he recognized the power of music in worship and he took advantage of it. He enjoyed the creative process, and music was an important part of that process. It was difficult (impossible?) to change Herman's mind. But I revelled in his determination. He really cared about that captive congregation and he used every ounce of his intellect and energy to make sure worship was vital, memorable and never boring:

> Blessed is the church whose members know and love one another. Blessed is the church where people worship and think and play together. Blessed is the church that is compassionate and daring in Christ's name. Blessed are you in this church when you walk with Christ. Rejoice and be exceeding glad, for great shall be your reward.
>
> (Benediction, date unknown)

The order of service was important to Herman. On one Sunday, he used a different order for his sermon "What's the Use of Going to Church?":

> Each part of the service has its own meaning. Choir members and ministers sit in nave pews at the start as a symbol that those who usually sit in the chancel are a part of and come from the congregation and are usually segregated in the chancel only in order to be better heard. The Words of Fellowship (announcements) are spoken from the floor of the nave, rather than from the chancel, not because they are unimportant in our coming together, but so that later on we can concentrate wholly on worship as such.
>
> At presentation of the offering, choir members, ushers and ministers face toward the Communion Table, as of course those in the nave pews always do. This is no "bit of superstition." A Communion Table, like the altar in some churches, is the center of the worship. All facing the Communion Table can be taken as a symbol of both our unity and our reverence for Christ, who is the host at the Table. The turning toward the Table is a physical expression of a spiritual humility and reverence.
>
> The benediction is said in unison as a way of symbolizing our Christian "togetherness," and also the Protestant principle that all church members are ministers of Christ, that each one can say "good words" to all the others.

(*Bene* in Latin means"good" and *dicta* means "words.") So we said good words to one another.

(Sermon, August 31, 1980)

Prayer

Herman had an unconventional attitude about prayer. In this "rumination," he debated the use of the words "Forgive us, Lord":

> I have long had a question about a sentence that occurs often in pastoral prayers or in prayers the congregation says in unison. After a recitation of some of our derelictions, the minister says, "Forgive us, Lord."
>
> Should not that "Forgive us, Lord" be examined? What is supposed to happen inside those who hear, or say, this prayer? Isn't it likely to be an expectation of cheap grace? Have we really felt sorry about the sins enumerated? Is such enumeration likely to be sincere? Would it not be better to pray something like this: "God, increase within us true sorrow for our misuse of life and assure us that you accept us, not waiting to give your love until we are as we ought to be. Let the assurance that you never leave us lift any crushing weight of guilt and empower us to move forward to better lives and a better day."
>
> Something like that seems to me more helpful than tossing off the plea, "Forgive us, Lord." I think the repeated use of that plea is evidence of spiritual indolence in those who use it, a series of words written down or spoken without full consent of mind and heart.
>
> Or, we might pray, after naming some of our derelictions: "God, are you still there? You have not gone away in disgust? You are still offering us your presence and your help? If you still, in spite of everything, care for us, we can have hope and courage for pushing on."
>
> (Rumination, November 22, 1982)

Herman expressed his concern about lengthy prayers in "How Should We Pray":

But, O those long, rambling prayers Jesus heard! They upset him. So he gave some advice: "In your prayers," he said, "do not go babbling on like the heathen, who imagine that the more they say the more likely they are to be heard. Do not imitate them. Your Father knows what your needs are before you ask him."

There is a time to pray and a time not to pray, or at least a time to stop praying and get on with the business. Meetings and church services in which someone says every few minutes, "Let us pray," are to some of us an affliction. As if the more we pray, the more we prove our piety. If you are praying alone, pray as long as you feel like it. If you are leading others in prayer, it should be remembered that they can follow you about so long and then the mind begins to wander, especially if the prayer is an assembly of random thoughts. A sermon or prayer without outline or clear progression is impossible to follow.

One of the most famous prayers ever used was a one-sentence prayer. It was first said by Reinhold Niebuhr, a true man of God and a great Christian theologian. The prayer has been copied and recopied. The U.S.O. distributed it to American soldiers. Alcoholics Anonymous adopted it. Recently I saw a framed copy in a doctor's office. This was the prayer: "O God, give us serenity to accept what cannot be changed, courage to change what should be changed, and wisdom to distinguish the one from the other."

I wish that in our churches we had more time for silent prayer. Ministers hesitate to ask the congregation to pray in silence, at least not long enough to let the silence become a living silence, because in any congregation there are many who don't know what to do with silence; they squirm and wonder how long this is going to last. It's a pity to lose the capacity for quiet meditation, when you just relax and let healing run through you. In my first year in the ministry, a physician told me that spiritual serenity is one of the first marks of greatness. The deeps of life, that is to say, God, speak to us saying, "O, be quiet."

Let us take an illustration from listening to a symphony orchestra. I suspect my own experience may be the experience of some of you. I read the program notes that describe the theme of a particular symphony, but usually, not being a musician, the notes do not help me much.

During the first ten minutes or so of the concert, I am a little restless. I am trying to be an active participant, trying to get my mind into the music. But, little by little, I find myself getting quiet inside, and by the middle of the concert something has happened to me. I am filled with a sense of well-being. The music has worked a change. I cannot rationalize it or understand it intellectually, but something has happened to me and that something is good. It is like a tide flowing in, covering rocks and dry sand. Something like this can be the result of worship and particularly of prayer.

Let us think about *The Lord's Prayer*. If Jesus or someone like him were to give us a prayer today, he would certainly not use the phrases we have in *The Lord's Prayer*. So, in order to make it a great prayer for ourselves now, we have to make the ancient words carry new and additional meanings.

(Sermon, March 4, 1973)

Almost twelve years later, Herman provided these new and additional meanings to *The Lord's Prayer* in his interpretation entitled "The Lord's Prayer Today":

Our Father/Mother God who art above, around and within us.	*Our Father who art in Heaven,*
Let your Being and your creation be be held in reverence.	*Hallowed be thy name.*
May we live more and more in love and mutual helpfulness, looking forward to the time when your purpose comes to fulfillment.	*Thy kingdom come.*
While we live on earth, let us not cease from the struggle to know and do your will in the Here and Now.	*Thy will be done on earth as it is in Heaven.*

May we strive unceasingly to provide food for all who live on earth.	*Give us this day, our daily bread.*
Let not our waywardness and foolishness build a wall between you and us or between us and our neighbors.	*Forgive us our debts as we forgive our debtors.*
Let your presence steer us away from temptations that may be too strong for us.	*And lead us not into temptation,*
Liberate us from the evil of self-serving aggression against the well- being of the earth and against our neighbors.	*But deliver us from evil.*
Not unto us but unto you, Creator, sustainer and friend, be all honor and glory.	*For thine is the kingdom and the power and the glory forever.*

(July 25, 1984)

Almost 40 years earlier, Herman wrote this prayer that was reproduced in several church calendars:

> Come, *my heart*, to Bethlehem. Follow the star through the night. Be not afraid to believe. See where he lies, the Truth which thou seekest, the Meaning of all thy weary striving. Behold, your King! Kneel before him, *who* has knelt before many false kings. Make room for him at last, *who* has sheltered the kings of hate and cruelty and greed. Here give thine adoration, *who* has worshipped gods who gave thee no blessing. To him give thy love, who has been betrayed and wounded.
>
> Kneel in humility, seeing that thy pride has brought only fear and pain. Surrender now, for he alone is unconquered and unconquerable. From thy wandering in barren wastes, come home to Bethlehem.

O my heart, thank God for his unspeakable gift. With all the choirs of heaven, sing Glory and Thanksgiving. Amen.

(December, 1945)

On a Christmas Eve 1974, at the candlelight service just before midnight, he prayed:

In this place of worship and in our homes we will be glad and take heart. For the love we receive and for the love we can give, for the dancing happiness in the eyes of children, for the thousand ways in which goodness and faith are shown among us, for these things and for much else we give thanks. When from the hour of singing we go back to the common life, let it be with more of the love and courage for which the world is hungry. We celebrate no dead event. He came and he comes. Tonight, tomorrow, through the days ahead, come to our hearts, Lord Jesus, melt some of our hardness, increase our sense of oneness with all that lives. Make each one of us a center of healing. Pull us back to where we belong. O come, my heart, adore, give thanks and live. Amen.

(December, 1974)

Worship as Dialogue

Herman prepared this Responsive Reading reflecting on "my country" during the days of heightened patriotism in World War II:

Leader: Who has decreed that *my country* shall include only the geographical area bounded by the Atlantic and Pacific Oceans, Canada, and Mexico? Who has decreed that *my country* shall embrace only those men, institutions, and events that lie between the year 1492 and the present?

Group: God help me to define *my country*.

Leader: Where Isaiah lifted up his voice for human justice, there is *my country*. Where Plato announced the reality of the spiritual, there is *my country*. Where St. Francis lived the compassionate life, there is *my country*.

Group: God help me to broaden my allegiance, not limiting it by little lines or by accidents of time and space.

Leader: Where Luther struck for the liberty of the soul, there is *my country*. Where Gandhi fights a swordless fight for freedom, there is *my country*. Where Schweitzer heals the bodies of the black man, there is *my country*. Where Kagawa champions the underprivileged, there is *my country*.

Group: God help me to own *my country* wherever men and women lift the flag of justice, or of beauty, or of freedom, or of truth, or of peace, or of fellowship.

(Reading, March 4, 1940)

The worshippers at a church service are not merely an audience. They participate as Herman explained in the sermon "What's the Use of Going to Church?":

In the coffee hour following the service, one worshipper expressed some puzzlement over my interpretation of worship as, in part, a dialogue between the worshipper and Jesus and the God of Jesus. Perhaps others felt some lack of clarity at this point.

Let us suppose you come into church feeling discouraged or depressed. You may not put it in words, but that is how you feel. That is your unverbalized part of the dialogue. Then, in anthem, hymn, Scripture reading, prayer, or sermon you can hear words of courage and faith. That, we can say, is God's part of the dialogue. He is responding to what you have said.

Or, let us suppose you feel guilty about something. This is what you are, in effect, "saying." Then you hear words about forgiveness, telling you that you are accepted by the Everlasting Mercy, no matter who or what you are. That is God's part of the dialogue.

Once more, you come into the church withdrawn into yourself, perhaps discontented because something is not the way you want it to be. That is what you are "saying." Now you hear at some point in the service words about the needs of others: the poor, the persecuted. Such words can be taken as God telling you to think of something else besides yourself.

In worship, you and I are saying something -- about the self or about the world around us, saying it without words but saying it nonetheless. And in real worship, God is saying something to us in response. You may, like Job, have an argument with God. All this means that the more honestly we look at ourselves, the more clear-eyed we look at our world and the more we know about Jesus and the kind of God we have, the more our worship becomes a lively dialogue.

(Sermon, August 31, 1980)

* * *

God bless Herman Reissig. I'll bet the discussions are lively.

Martha B. Porter, photographer

"Reasoning can never be conclusive; finally one must take a leap of trust."

Chapter V. FAITH

Edited by the Rev. R. Alan Johnson,
Secretary of Evangelism and Membership Growth,
United Church Board for Homeland Ministries,
United Church of Christ

Herman Reissig was preoccupied with faith. He invited his readers and listeners over and again to explore, to challenge and even to affirm a faith that made sense and makes sense of things.

His faith was dynamic, alive and becoming. Like the Old Testament character, Jacob, Herman was a God-wrestler. He grappled intellectually with the living presence of "something or Someone that means good, means it persistently and that is finally invincible."

In many ways Herman sought, like Jacob, to name this presence, though he also felt this task to be impossible without distortion. In a letter to me he complained that "we have to use religious words in order to convey the realities of religion. I shy away from even using *God* too much. There is no juice in it." Yet, as Jacob persisted through the night until the morning and then received his name and, though wounded, got up and went on, so Herman would "think and think and reason and reason and argue and argue and then admit that reasoning can never be conclusive, that finally one must make a leap of trust."

Herman invited us to share with him a doubting faith and a faithful doubt. His penetrating questions cut to the core of issues and invited, almost demanded, response. The exchange was energizing -- indeed, compelling -- in pulpit, forum, Second Hour, or letter. He was a quintessential faith-wrestler.

Sermons and letters written throughout a 12-year friendship form the basis for this chapter on Herman's struggle for faith. In the course of his own struggle, he wanted to update, to stimulate and to provoke everyone within ear-shot and postal service.

Faith and Doubt: The Boundary Line

Herman always struggled; a firm faith never came easily for him:

> I do live on the boundary between belief and unbelief. And, this is where many of our church members live, often without being aware of it. Since I often push at the boundary, this helps to give my preaching whatever little imprint it has.
>
> (Letter, September 2, 1977)

He wrote and preached as an interpreter from this boundary line. After a re-reading of the gospel of Mark, he wrote:

> I felt again the immense gulf between the modern way of thinking and how people felt and talked in the pre-scientific time. Not that I want to be limited to reason and logic. But if there are more things under the sun than reason knows of, I still cannot, with any sense of reality, use the terms and images that were real to people in Biblical times. I suspect that our continuing use of Biblical images and stories, without interpretations, encourages skepticism instead of faith. Our people may listen with a "devout" face, but under the surface of their minds they must be resisting and rebelling.
>
> (Letter, December 13, 1978)

How the rebel, the God-wrestler, in Herman loved to get under the surface of our minds, disturbing mushy or rigid faith! This honest inquiry attracted people of all ages to him. Faith for Herman did not mean covering up what is too difficult to face. It meant uncovering our difficulty in believing and dealing with it. "I have never had," he wrote, "what some Christians apparently do have --an undisturbed sureness about the reality and the love of God."

Herman's own far-ranging quest lent credibility to our own search beyond church doctrine for what is true and real. He acknowledged that new discoveries, contemporary experience and potential hazards posed provocative new challenges.

Asserting that faith "untested in the light of these is not a faith at all, but a sign of spiritual vacuity," he wrote in his sermon, "A Question About Evangelism and Church Community":

> What is to be done? We are, to put it bluntly, in a "bind." In Christianity, being an historical religion, we cannot disregard our roots as they are given us in the Bible. The roots are entangled in a dead culture. There is no possibility of making that culture come alive in modern minds, no matter how much we explain. Twentieth-century people cannot think like first or second, or even like 13th century people. Matthew Arnold wrote in *Dover Beach*:
>
> *The sea of faith*
> *Was once, too, at the full, and round earth's shore*
> *Lay like the folds of a bright girdle furled.*
> *But now I only hear*
> *Its melancholy, long, withdrawing roar,*
> *Retreating, to the breath*
> *Of the night-wind, down the vast edges drear*
> *And naked shingles of the world.*
> *Ah, love, let us be true to one another!*
> *For the world, which seems*
> *To lie before us like a land of dreams,*
> *So various, so beautiful, so new,*
> *Hath really neither joy, nor love, nor light,*
> *Nor certitude, nor peace, nor help for pain;*
> *And we are here as on a darkling plain*
> *Swept with confused alarms of struggle and flight,*
> *Where ignorant armies clash by night.*
>
> When Arnold wrote these prophetic lines the conditions that attack the red corpuscles of faith and produce spiritual anemia were just beginning their onslaught. Later came the new biology, the new psychology, the Niagara of technical invention, the new chemistry and the new physics.
>
> Later still, in the present century, came the time of holocaust, two ghastly world wars, the Great Depression,

Auschwitz, Hiroshima, Vietnam and the prospect of universal death in atomic war. This is the intellectual and spiritual climate in which contemporary people struggle for meaning.

(Sermon, October 25, 1980)

The sermon, "What Does It Mean to Believe in God?", captured Herman's anguish of searching for the ultimate:

My God is no off-earth potentate, making rules, alternately sweet and harsh. My God suffers with us, feels our agony, dies on a cross, languishes in prisons, weeps at hospital beds. My God lures, invites, pulls and pushes -- and, being God, does not give up. Will God win? We might begin over again, on this earth or on another planet. But I join with the millions who don't want all that we have built and achieved turned into poisoned ashes through human folly, and therefore I join with the millions crying, "Stop this insane notion that you are going to save with atomic weapons anything worth saving!"

My God does not ask for praise. We don't think highly of a man or woman who is always looking for compliments. Praise is good for us, for as the poet said, "We needs must love and praise the highest when we see it." But God's desire must be that we do justice and love mercy and help one another. My God wants us to align ourselves with a moving toward justice and mutual aid. My God is a great magnet that keeps drawing me back toward his purposes, especially when I want to enjoy myself and let the world go hang.

(Sermon, October 9, 1983)

(The full text of this sermon can be found in Appendix I.)

Uneasily In Love With God

Herman begged us "not to let the blood go out of our words." In "My Life at Eighty-Two," he preached:

The best I can do when it comes to faith is something like this: There is a possibility that life has an ultimate meaning behind the capacity of the human mind to understand or prove, that *Something, Someone* is ultimately in charge, that our little meanings add up to ultimate meaning. I try, therefore, to put my life on that side, trusting that even if I and all others come to a complete end of self-consciousness when we die, I should still try to live as richly and helpfully as possible. Years ago my late wife, Bun, said to me, "You strike me as a person uneasily in love with God." That says it pretty well.

(Sermon, October 27, 1981)

(Editor's note: The metaphor is a conscious reference to the epitaph of Robert Frost, requested by the poet for his own gravestone in Bennington, Vermont: "He was uneasily in love with the world.")

Herman often used the word "uneasy" to describe his view from the boundary:

Some observant person is going to dub me "Mr. Uneasy." I have now preached sermons on "Uneasily in Love with God," "Uneasily in Love with America," and "Uneasily in Love with the Church." But isn't that what a Christian is supposed to be, even with respect to God?

(Letter, May 20, 1975)

His "signature" sermon, "Uneasily in Love with God" (from which this book takes its title), is among the first sermons Herman preached at First Congregational Church in Old Greenwich:

The purpose of this sermon is to help persons with two different kinds of spiritual problems: those who have great difficulty believing in the essential goodness of life -- which is to say, in God -- because in our world there is so much pain, injustice and seeming irrationality, and those,on the other hand, whose faith is not as robust as it could be because they believe too easily. There must be some in both groups here this morning.

Now we are ready for the uneasy part. Friend, if you believe without question in a benevolent providence that oversees all things and watches over us with love, if your love for God is never shaken, you believe too easily.

Thomas Hardy summed up the truth of the matter in two lines:

If a way to the better there be
It exacts a full look at the worst.

And John Calvin, the Protestant reformer, put it bluntly: "He who never has a doubt is a fool."

You find it easy to love a good God and to be confident? Where have you been? For some of us the worst blow that love for a loving God has had to take was not a personal loss but the deliberate extermination of five million Jews in a few years under the Hitler regime. Go and stand before the mass graves at the extermination camp near Munich, look at the gas chambers, ovens and gallows. A mind-searching horror. You believe easily in a good and omnipotent God?

It is when we have looked at the worst, been honest about our own muddled selves, faced the devil in us, been bowed down by human waywardness and suffering, and have worked our way through it that faith and love acquire lift and power. As an old Russian proverb puts it, "The darker the night, the clearer the stars." Without suffering, especially spiritual suffering, there is no faith worth talking about.

The truly spiritual person has flung his faith into the teeth of the storm. It is when you and I have wrestled with God and the devil, heaven and hell, good and evil, faith and despair, that we may achieve spiritual serenity and spiritual power.

(Sermon, July 29, 1973)

In Herman's own search, there was also some deep assurance to be found:

I, like my sisters and brothers, seem to have had implanted in me a core of hope and faith that remains solid even when I am uncertain about or positively reject most traditional theological doctrines.

(Letter, February 24, 1978)

There are only for us poor mortals hints, gleams and maybe some hours when we are overwhelmed with the assurance that there is here a Presence and a Power that will not be defeated. It really comes down to *faith*, doesn't it? One makes a decision, risks one's life -- despite all the failure and suffering. I am working this out for myself and it will probably get into my Easter sermon. "If you want proof, you will never believe." That at least I can say to myself and to the congregation. Great Christians have always been great risk-takers.

(Letter, February 24, 1980)

Jesus

The declaration of faith in a God who is intimately personal continued to elude Herman. He wrestled with that relationship and reported, near the end of his life:

I still do not know how to fit the idea of God as a supreme personal being in what we are now learning about this vast universe. . . I am putting my faith in a Holy Spirit. And God the Son, Jesus, tells me what the Holy Spirit is doing. My description of Jesus of Nazareth is as the "local presence of God."

(Letter, October 28, 1983)

In Jesus of Nazareth, Herman found the focus of a faith which enlivens and empowers, as he stated in his sermon, "My Life at Eighty-Two":

I think much about the kind of person Jesus was. I am deeply drawn to his amazing integrity, dealing with life. I can address a prayer to "the Spirit of the Living Christ." I try to hang on to that Spirit, seeing it as alive in our world, even if far, far from regnant. My lapses from honesty and from loving seem to me a betrayal of him. A man who goes to church every Sunday and whom I know well, said to me that Jesus is not a "real" person to him. He is real to me. And despite all the difficulties with the documents (in the New Testament), it is certain that there was such a man and that we can have an authentic picture of the kind of man he was.

(Sermon, October 27, 1981)

Herman read voraciously in modern scholarship about the person of Jesus. He read and re-read with special eagerness *Jesus, an Experiment in Christology*, by E. Schillebeeckx.

With all the difficulties in the Gospel accounts, I seem to get a fairly clear picture of the essence of Christ and to that essence I will cling. I need something to pull life together and I know of nothing and no one that more fully commands my mind and my heart. As I said in last Sunday's sermon, "With Christ as my center, I cannot be sure of every step, but I know my direction." As to "very God of very God," I will say only: it is my faith that he speaks from out of the heart of life. And this is pure faith -- nothing that I can prove.

(Letter, December 13, 1978)

Jesus did not let Herman go, and Herman did not let go of Jesus. The power of the One whom Herman knew in the Christ continued to feed and fuel his faith. In his sermon, "Human Being: Wonderful, Vulnerable," he speaks of Jesus' full humanity:

Don't we all feel that we have thus far only a little hint of what love can be? So now, in this life, this wonderful life, you will try to be more fully human,won't you? And, if you are not sure what being fully human means, keep your eyes on Jesus of Nazareth. See his love, his self-giving, his courage, his faith! This is what we are meant to be.

(Sermon, February 19, 1984)

Christ and Social Justice

For Herman, the way of Christ may bring us into conflict with some other ways as he expressed in his sermon,"Singing the Lord's Song In A Foreign Land."

> The President says. . . the Pentagon says. . . We will listen, but Christians march to the sound of a different drum. If you and I do not intend, in public as well as in private matters, to take Jesus of Nazareth seriously, it would be better to be honest and stop going to church. Clearly what we Americans are doing today in many areas, but especially in the arms race, is not Christ's way. Like those ancient Hebrews in Babylon, we are exiles. Or, if you think the word "exile" is too strong, we must at least feel the tension, an almost agonizing tension, between our religion and the way our world thinks and acts. Translate the old poet's words like this: "If I do not remember Christ, may my Christian words stick in my throat."
>
> (Sermon, May 6, 1984)

This sermon received the 1987 Connecticut Conference Peace Center Preaching Award, awarded posthumously. (The full text can be found in Appendix I.)

In a lecture "What Are We Here For?" he continued this theme:

> Let us not worry too much about theological concepts. Let us concentrate on living responsibly with love and justice in our dealings with one another. On that road, the God who seems to hide from us in our time may once more reappear. We may meet the living God when we, in love, meet our neighbors. There is no way to love God, no way at all, except in loving the world of created things and especially my own life and my neighbors.
>
> (Lecture, March 18, 1973)

Herman had little patience for any who would mouth a faith of platitudes:

> Said a successful manufacturer to me -- he was in church every Sunday -- "When you go into business you might as well forget about Christian principles." No one acquainted with the world of business and politics imagines that we can

take what we hear on Sunday into those areas and easily make it work. *But* a purely private religion that avoids the great social questions is, in the end, a truncated religion that denies the Lordship of Christ over all of life.

(Letter, April 24, 1980)

Herman's faith did not go with the prevailing winds of opinion:

It seems to be true that American corporations doing business in Latin America are working with a small minority of the powerful and rich in those countries in ways that enrich the corporations and the native minority and that keep the majority in poverty. (Cf. A *Theology of Liberation* by Guiterrez and *Theology in a New Key* by Robert McAfee Brown.) American corporation executives do not see this and they are not likely to applaud anyone who calls it to their attention. Yet if Christians are to be concerned about the poor they have to face and change such facts. Is a minister who sees the actual situation justified in keeping quiet about it? If corporation officers are in his (her) congregation, the temptation to stay away from such unpalatable truths is very great.

(Letter, September 2, 1979)

Herman proposed this mock versicle and response for more honest public worship:

Tell it to the nations? ("Keep out of politics, please.")
Tell it to the corporations? ("Mind your own business.")
Tell it to the Washington Administration? ("Don't you criticize my President!")

(Sermon, October 21, 1973)

When the *Readers Digest* sharply criticized the World Council of Churches for statements and grants for social justice in the Third World, Herman wrote:

In contrast to what the churches, Catholic and Protestant, did for centuries, our Christian leaders (the Catholic Bishops and leaders of the World and National Councils of Churches) today are trying, like Jesus, to speak for the poor and the hungry; to speak for justice. I find little evidence that writers of *Readers Digest* articles have made a serious study of the New Testament.

In Spain and Latin America the change began, not in the hierarchy, but with priests who lived with the poor. This movement led finally to what is called "liberation theology." The change had, in essence, nothing to do with Marxism; it had everything to do with a rediscovery of the prophets and of Jesus, who in his ministry stood solidly with the disinherited, the outcasts, the poor.

Neither Catholic bishops nor Protestant teachers any longer see validity in the admonition to "stick to religion and leave politics alone." Peace among the nations, questions of housing, work, land ownership, race relations, corporate business policies impinge on the whole life of every person and are therefore the concern of the followers of Jesus Christ.

(Rumination, November 22, 1982)

One of Herman's great delights was in disturbing the quieted waters:

I feel a little sinful satisfaction in having said in the sermon as delivered, "President Reagan says the situation in South Africa is getting better. Bishop Tutu says it is getting worse. The bishop is right; the president is wrong." That may be the first time Reagan has been criticized from our pulpit – and it was about time. No one walked out.

(Letter, December 17, 1984)

He was in no way obsequious in raising questions about our racial composition:

Somehow a church where, with respect to color, only one-third of the human race is represented doesn't feel right, or let's say it doesn't feel as good as a church not limited to one race. If you suspect you have in you some lurking feeling of being superior because you are white, even against Chinese or Japanese, pray God for the grace to repent and be saved. This church imposes no racial limitation to membership. Our problem is that the racial composition of the community makes us a white people's church.

(Sermon, March 27, 1977)

A serious Christian cannot feel at home in our political-economic order, with its overwhelming emphasis on competition, personal upward mobility and the profit motive.

(Letter, September 15, 1984)

Herman prodded his listeners to the point of discomfort as in this sermon, "What Shapes Your Life?":

Let's take his most shocking example and teaching, that about turning the other cheek, and set it in the middle of our hardest contemporary problem, the piling up of nuclear weapons. Another one of my correspondents in this church sent me a copy of the distinguished British publication, *The Economist*. In a long, carefully-reasoned editorial, *The Economist* examines the arms race and, particularly, the proposals in the letter by Catholic bishops. The writer thinks the bishops are mistaken. He says: "Turning the other cheek is good when other cheeks are also ready to turn. Until then, the owner of the unturned cheek has his way; vigorous bad beats passive good, and the world becomes a worse place."

So much for Jesus Christ. His teaching,along with his cross -- dismissed! Politely, even a little sadly dismissed, but still dismissed. Too bad, fellow! We will put your cross in our churches and sing about the cross, but no cross for us, please, especially not for our nation. We know a better way: "To have peace, prepare for war." That's the true wisdom. We can cite history to prove it. To be sure, that history turns out to be a story of endless fighting and preparation for fighting, but we intend to go right on with killing and preparing to kill. Jesus, you were just plain naive, simplistic, utopian. You didn't understand the real world.

Nevertheless, I can think of no question that faces us today on which Jesus Christ does not have something important to say. We should not, of course, try in wooden, literal manner to follow him. Christian living requires thinking. The question for us is, Will we take our Christ seriously? Do we come to church to hear the world's wisdom reflected in song and sermon, or do we come to listen to another drumbeat?

(Sermon, March 31, 1983)

We listened to "another drumbeat" when it came through Herman, because he was never arrogant in the way he said things. He was never far from this confession:

At least occasionally I bring myself up short by saying to myself, "O you *preacher*! You always think of taking some stirring word into the pulpit. You should first ask how you can take it into your own life." Is not that the insidious temptation of us preachers? I should say to myself, "Preacher, first live. Then preach."

(Letter, February 17, 1984)

New Horizons

Herman's understanding continued to expand. He grew in appreciation of the voices in theological discourse that encourage inclusive language, for example, the use of more than the male pronouns for the descriptions of God. In one fanciful verse he wrote:

We assumed that God is a he;
The women ask, "Why not a she?"
The truth now dawns on the masculine clod:
Tis clear we have an androgynous God.

Even as he wrote his own version of *The Lord's Prayer,* Herman began,"Our Father/Mother God." (Text is in Chapter IV,

"Worship.") Instead of repeating doctrinal definitions of God, Herman's credo-sermon "This I Believe" ended:

> Gather up the demand and struggle for justice, the reality and necessity of love, the push toward truth, the possibility of triumph over suffering and evil -- gather such things together and give them a name. The name is God.
>
> (September 28, 1974)

Herman's faith was rich with gut-wrenching questions as shown in his sermon "On Being Converted":

> Often in our liberal Protestant church services, so rational and careful, dignified to the point of leaving us as cold as a day in winter, I hunger for something that will shake and grip me, make me see what a poor thing I have made of my life and lift me to a higher level. Something is missing in a religion that doesn't at least set the mind to dancing. And, if we should also dance with our feet or parade around the church, well, why not? Why should we think we must limit ourselves to the cool processes of the mind? As if we could be alive to God only from the neck up? While we think we are admirably rational, we may be only refrigerated.
>
> For here is the hidden danger: many of us baptized, confirmed and church-going persons have not for years been grasped by a fresh insight or been spiritually shook up, repeatedly playing the same record.
>
> (Sermon, March 6, 1977)

Perseverance

In spite of the struggle and faith-wrestling with the conditions of the world, Herman wrote:

> If I were writing my autobiography, I might speak of the frequency of my sense of personal defeat and of the reasons or the manner of the defeats. Here I will only say that many years ago I began saying to myself in those bad hours, "Get up and go on!" I had given up the hope of attaining a steadily

virtuous life, such as one dreams about when young. Being always what is called "good" was not for me. What then? The answer was, when I slipped and fell, to say to myself, "Get up and go on!" And I did. The result has been that there have been many more good and strong hours than weak and bad hours. I have been one who, in Browning's word, "always walks breast forward." (Or almost always.)

It occurred to me years ago that, although this slogan may sound quite a-religious, it could be interpreted, in my case at least, as the grace of God. I was given the grace to say, *Get up and go on!*

(Letter, September 26, 1979)

Herman was constantly reading which provided this blessing and commissioning:

This morning I felt glum. Then, having been on my knees for awhile (washing the kitchen floor), I picked up Kirk's biography of Pablo Casals. Kirk quotes Casals in his 97th year, three months before he died, speaking during a concert in Central Park: "I am an old man, but in many senses a young man. And this is what I want you to be: young, young in all your life, and to say things to the world that are true."

That, to me, was as much a word from the Lord as any prophet ever heard. So I have ceased from being glum. My friend, be young all your life and say things to the world that are true.

(Letter, May 24, 1974)

Helen S. Allen, Artist

"In most of our 'liberal' churches, there is no thunder at all, the preaching is all too soft, accommodating and genial and optimistic."

Chapter VI. PREACHING AND THE BIBLE

Edited by the Rev. R. Alan Johnson, and
Betty and Harry Woodman, parishioners,
First Congregational Church of Greenwich,
Old Greenwich, Connecticut

PREACHING

Herman Reissig took preaching seriously. He ranked preaching as Number One among a minister's responsibilities. He often stated that a minister, above all, owed his congregation a good sermon.

The thought that he put into preaching is demonstrated in his extensive correspondence. Herman did not prepare a sermon in a set time period. It was an ongoing thought process that may have started months or even years before the sermon and did not stop until the dialogue through conversations and correspondence, and his own further ruminations, ended some weeks after the sermon delivery.

Reflections in Letters

Herman's thoughts on preaching are best expressed in these excerpts from letters written to some of his regular correspondents:

> I said to mine Adorable One that, making allowances for your exuberant spirit, your comment that I "get inside of people" is just about the best tribute a sermon could have. To get inside people -- and not to read them an essay, that's the aim of preaching. Will I do it next Sunday in Old Greenwich, when I try to explain and commend Christian social action? There could be so many ways of talking about this and I have almost never had to wrestle so hard with a subject, writing

and rewriting the thing to make it lucid and perhaps a little moving. And so many different attitudes in that congregation.

(April 2, 1975)

Which reminds me to suggest a text for you. No copyright on this, although I think the next sermon I write will use it. Psalm 77:3 "I think of God and I moan." (RSV) Imagine it! According to liberal religion, he should have written, "I think of God and feel good." But this guy looked at the God of righteousness and then at the awful unrighteousness around him and he could only moan. There's a theme for us morally obtuse, or nonchalant moderns. The sermon could be titled, "When Man Thinks of God." Or, perhaps, the sermon should combine the two foci of our faith: judgment and forgiveness. But to preach on these two basics is not easy -- not easy to avoid a self-righteous tone or merely to point out the obvious and grosser iniquities and then to make the forgiveness too easy. Still, we (including us preachers) do need to be shaken up, but not to the point of despair.

(April 2, 1975)

The members of the Club of Rome are serious people. They have concluded that we have to have a virtual Copernican change in our values -- if we are to survive. I agree. Now here is the assignment for theologians and preachers: these men and women do not speak of God or providence or sin and judgment. They assume that human beings will have to put their heads together and make the necessary decisions. And what these Club of Rome people say on a high intellectual level -- *with* the aid of computers -- most of the people we preach to *assume* without putting it into words. There is here just an awfully big gap between the modern person's everyday assumptions and what we say in church.

I think we should expose the gap, describing as honestly as we can the modern "scientific," rational way of thinking and then the Biblical concepts and then asking if the two can somehow be reconciled and how. Of course a lot of this sort of thing has been done by writers and preachers, but not nearly as honestly and thoroughly as called for.

This question suggests the book I would like to write. But I have to say that such a book would require far more learning than I have, as well as a couple of years of hard work. The best I can do is to work out some aspects of the question in sermons.

(July 18, 1975)

Here is a typical homiletic illustration you may have for nothing. Yesterday, walking along a street in the heat, I felt no tiniest bit of breeze. But, looking up, I saw that the tops of the trees were restless, waving back and forth. The conscious mind is driven back and forth by the currents of life. But down beneath, the trunk stands steady because its roots go deep into the earth. I think I will use this, or something like it, for an introduction to my next pastoral prayer. It is good, I think, to use a sentence or two as introduction, instead of just "Let us pray."

(July 20, 1977)

I have just finished the first volume of Pauck's biography of Tillich. I think Pauck has written with a wonderful combination of realism, grace and appreciation. A great book, which stirs the mind. Pauck quotes with approval what a friend of Tillich said of him: "a saintly demon and a demonic saint." One of Tillich's favorite phrases, "Living on the boundary" is a seminal idea (boundary between philosophy and theology, etc.,etc.). Also between pessimism and hope, belief and unbelief. With only a fragment of Tillich's erudition and brilliance, I have much in common with the man.

(September 2, 1977)

I have a word for you and for me and for all preachers, a word to be inscribed in letters of fire in the preacher's study and by which he should measure the worth of any subject he plans to develop in a sermon. The word comes from Ernst Bloch, the erudite Marxist and profound student of religion who was as little at home in Stalinesque communism as in orthodox theology and whose book *Man Alone* I have just read for the second time, with a constant excitement and fertilization of the mind. Bloch wrote:

> *Though religion may have got on splendidly with ignorance and even with stupidity, it never got on with triviality.*

I more than blush, I blanch to think how many of my sermons have, relative to the great themes, been trivial – interesting enough perhaps and not wholly without value, but still not worth the precious 25 minutes of pulpit time. Homiletic tidbits, no more.

Wherefore, the once-a-month sermons I have planned for the next seven months will deal with subjects too great for me. This is not to say that there will be nothing of an immediate and "practical" nature in the sermons. It is to say that the immediate and the practical should issue from the profoundest themes, and not from the top of the contemporary mind. Even so, the sermon will not be as evanescent as many sermons, including mine, have been.

(March 31, 1978)

Perhaps we get close to the fundamental question by asking: Is there a moral order that man did not create? We must not answer this question too easily. If we can still say, "Thus saith the Lord," how can we say it so that the modern mind can believe it?

I think modern prophets can still thunder, but they certainly cannot persuasively do it à la Jonathan Edwards. And in most of our liberal churches, there is no thunder at all; the preaching is all too soft, accommodating and genial and optimistic.

(Undated)

Listening to sermons, my friends, is for a lot of people a kind of sanctified entertainment. But I guess it is not up to you and me to change them. Enough that, by thinking and searching and praying, we change ourselves, hoping that our words will help a little to let God get in and do the changing:

Through the night of doubt and sorrow
Onward goes the pilgrim band,
Singing songs of expectation,
Marching to the promised land.

(April 3, 1978)

I have been thinking about your suggestion that the sermon might have offered ways to help the poor. You suggested, as I recall, only direct giving of food. I agree we should do this. But my social action background inclines me more toward thinking about the political and economic structural change that will help the poor to help themselves.

(November 22, 1978)

Advice to Ministers

In a letter to a new minister giving advice about preaching, Herman gave these pearls of wisdom:

If you are an old-fashioned preacher, or a sleep-inducing preacher, you will spend the first quarter or the first half of the sermon examining what repentance and forgiveness mean in Luke-Acts and then you would tack on a few generalized exhortations to your congregation to *repent* and accept forgiveness. If, like Jesus, you are less interested in what was said and thought by "them of old time" than in trying to meet the actual needs of your people, you will, at the beginning or in the middle or near the end of the sermon, explicate what repentance and forgiveness meant *then*, but spend 95% of the time bringing guilt (felt or needing-to-be-felt) to the surface and helping your people to deal with it in a way that heals.

The above is only a roundabout way of saying, what Fosdick used to emphasize, that people do not come to church avid for an accurate account of what Moses or Paul said, but wanting help in dealing with themselves and their world *now*. Of course, you prove that you understand this in your final comments on the relevance of repentance and forgiveness in pastoral counselling, and no more in preaching than in counselling should a minister *begin* with the Bible, although she/he will get a lot of help there.

(Letter, December 11, 1982)

In an installation service, Herman commented upon the importance of how the English language is used:

First, do, please, be a respecter and lover of the English language. In our use of English, most of us are like a cook who indolently sticks to the same tiresome dishes. Your objective is to build a conduit through which the truth, insight, vision that has seized you will flow into the living persons sitting in the pews. The conduit is made of words. When you have written a sermon, go back over it and ask yourself it if is not possible to say this or that in a more interesting and incisive way. Many words are plain tired; they droop and sag, have lost all their sap. Wear out a thesaurus of English words and phrases about once every ten years. Startle your hearers with a word they did not expect.

Reinhold Niebuhr, lecturing or preaching, often made people laugh. Not by telling a joke, which he never did, and not, oh certainly not, by being cute. They laughed because he had put a thought in such deliciously exact words. As when, for example, he said: "The trouble with dissoluble marriages is that they produce indissoluble children."

(Installation, May 5, 1974)

In this ordination "Charge," he had one of his most eloquent moments:

My dear friend, now you're in for it! That is to say, you are committed. You, of course, committed yourself long before you came to this church this afternoon, only now you've gone public with it. Your sister and brother ministers have laid their hands on your head saying, by so doing, an eloquent "Amen." Your family has also given you their assent. It occurs to me we have done just about everything except having a plane do some skywriting.

Congregationalists compensate for their theological free-thinking by insisting on certain quaint traditional customs such as requiring that the ordinand be charged by someone who presumably has earned the right to give advice. You have asked me to charge you. I am *not* going to do it! I don't feel up to it. Instead, let us just think together for a few minutes about what it means to be ordained. My interpretation will not conflict with the solemn words and promises of the ceremony of a few minutes ago. It will only be a little less dignified. After all, you can't live all the time on the high level of this church. You have to tend to household chores and yard work and call the plumber, and in any church you serve, you will have to deal with a lot of very earthy things, including perhaps jousting with church officers who obstinately refuse to see the light.

Well, so let us think first about what ordination does *not* mean. It does not mean that suddenly you have been given a unique amount of personal goodness. You are as good now as you were when you came to church this afternoon and *not a bit gooder*. We preachers talk so much about goodness and God that we are insidiously and unknowingly tempted to think we are the good we talk about, and even that maybe we have more of the image of God than other people. An ordination does not give you the right to preach the word, administer the Sacrament, while other Christians do not have the right. The Reformation doctrine of the priesthood of all believers means, among other things, that any Christian can preach the word and any sincere Christian can do a valid baptism, and pray over the bread and the wine. As for marrying people, that right is given to you by the State, not the church. Judges and justices of the peace have the right to pronounce a woman and a man wife and husband, so what does ordination mean? I think the difference lies here. You *purposefully* and *constantly* think about the great issues of life that most people think about only occasionally and briefly. You are ordained to be a *researcher* in what it means to be human, what it means to believe in God. Others read the Bible, you read it more constantly and closely. In short, you are a specialist in the meaning and purpose of human existence. You read the newspaper and the book that other people read but you read it with an *angle*. You read it *sub speciae aeternitas* -- "in the light of the eternal."

Well, this is a thrilling, absorbing, never-ending task. You will be concerned about bread, especially since so many millions of people in our world do not have enough bread, but you are especially impressed with the truth of the old aphorism that "human beings do not live by bread alone." This to me is the meaning of ordination. In a word, you are ordained to be what every human being is ordained to be, *only more so*.

The next question is, how are you and I going to keep it up? How are you and I, in this world, where "ignorant armies clash by night" and by day, where faith, hope and love are assaulted by cynicism and brutal selfishness, going to go on day after day, year after year believing, hoping, loving? Well! I am conscious all the time that I am not telling you anything you don't know. I am only emphasizing it. This is where faith comes in; just faith, no proof, no final victories, just faith. And faith, what's that? It is *not* giving assent to everything in the creeds or liturgies. I have more questions about God than you can shake a stick at, but somehow from somewhere, I have what I call a *core* confidence. It is the confidence that, despite all the evidence to the contrary, and despite my own weakness, there is *something* or *someone* here that means good and means it with persistence and is invincible.

For keeping and nurturing this core confidence, you and I can get help from many sources. We can get it from men and women whose names will never get into the history books. Some of them will be in your church. We can get it from heroic persons, such as Abraham Lincoln, Mahatma Ghandi and Martin Luther King. Most of all, to speak personally, I get it from the man, Jesus of Nazareth. I study that *stunning* awesome integrity, that resolute love, that courage born of love and I say: For me, *this is it*! I will take my stand with him. If Jesus was a fool, I will be a fool with him. I don't feel strong every day. Sometimes I feel horribly weak and want to quit, but this Christ persists right through the unspeakably horrible cross. Oh! What courage! Wholly unintimidated! If faith in God results in such love, courage and persistence, *this* must be the *meaning* of that central Biblical assertion: *God is love*.

So, you are on your way. With a deep and quiet joy and with an equally deep confidence, I salute you.

(Ordination Charge, September 18, 1983)

THE BIBLE

Herman Reissig felt strongly that the Bible should not be read literally. The Bible reflects the thinking of a former time and does not always reflect contemporary life. He expressed some of these views in the column "Something to Think About" which he wrote for *The Ledger*, Lakeland, Florida in the early 1970s. Here are some excerpts from these columns:

Constitution and the Bible

The Constitution has a central core that, hopefully, will not change; and that gives the United States a special character, but, also, the document is flexible enough to make it adaptable to new situations. Without this flexibility, permitting new interpretations by the Court, the Constitution could not serve a growing, changing nation.

Between the Constitution and the Bible there is at least one interesting and significant parallel. Both have a core of what might loosely be called infallibility. Flexible as it is, one cannot read just anything into the Constitution. It permits neither dictatorship nor anarchy, neither rule by minority nor unchallengeable rule by a majority. If it does not provide for pure democracy, it comes down emphatically on the side of the democratic idea.

So also, despite different levels of reliability and insight into the Bible, leading to many interpretations, the book has a central core that cannot be ignored or denied. Here are some of the principal Biblical emphases: the immeasurable worth of the human person; the tragic tendency toward a self-defeating egoism (sin), on the one side, and the capacity for nobility and altruism, on the other; concern for the neighbor, whatever the neighbor's nation or race; love as the goal and final law of life; the ever-present possibility of new life (resurrection); one humanity under God; the transiency of evil and the final victory of the good; the meaning and destiny of life (God), supremely revealed in Jesus of Nazareth.

The test of any interpretation of the Constitution is its harmony with the great ends of justice, welfare and freedom. The test of any part of the Bible is its harmony with the core emphases I have mentioned. If we use the Bible to support something foolish or harmful, we do it only by lifting a particular statement or story out of the context of the whole book. And those who insist on a "strict construction" of the Constitution should study the whole document, especially the statement of its purposes in the Preamble.

(© *The Ledger*, September 2, 1972)

Evolution or Genesis Story

We are compelled to choose. Either every reputable biologist in the world and every first-class anthropologist makes the biggest mistake science has ever made, or the Genesis account is a moving attempt to explain the world's and man's origins but is not to be taken as history. The story is indeed poetry -- poetry of the sublimest kind. It is more than poetry. When it says, "In the beginning God . . ." the story makes an assertion no scientist is in a position to dispute and that no real scientist attempts to dispute. And when we are told that human beings share "the image of God," we can humbly respond, "Amen," and bet our lives on the truth of the assertion.

The way to honor this part of the Bible is to accept its spiritual message but not try to turn the details into reliable history. For if all the statements in the first two chapters tell us what actually occurred, then we must make the same conclusion about the third chapter, which gives us the story of the Fall. Here we have a talking snake and a man and a woman hiding themselves in the garden so that God Almighty cannot find them! To insist that this is real history is irresponsible folly. In the story of the Fall, as in the account of creation, there is profound spiritual insight. Science does not discredit the insight. Those who insist on verbal infallibility are the ones who bring the whole story into disrepute, leading intelligent people to dismiss the whole because the details so clearly cannot be true.

To those who, in the name of Biblical defense, want to ban the teaching of evolution one wants to say: "O you of little faith!" Their faith is small because they fear to admit any error in the Bible lest they lose the whole Bible. Such an attitude is neither reason nor faith. The Bible needs no defense. Theories of its infallibility, as if every syllable were straight from the mind of God, are expressions of human insecurity and fear. Those ministers of religion who know this are, to put it plainly, derelict in not helping their people to read the book for what it is -- a truly great and indispensable witness to undying truth, a book as human as it is divine, not to be read as the final explanation of everything or as truth without human flaw.

(©*The Ledger*, February 17, 1973)

Bible: Incredibly Rich Book

Preachers and lay Bible readers have seemed to say that every word in the book is final and unchangeable truth. And this seems to mean that one can open the Bible to any page, put his finger on any verse and find something infallibly true and incomparably valuable.

But this is an impossible position. Impossible, not because "liberals" or scientists say so, but because the Bible does not always agree with itself. The Bible does not always agree with itself because the revelation, or, as some would say, the discovery of God and of his ways with men is progressive. It moves from very primitive to higher and purer conceptions.

. . . . .

In addition to the Bible's recording of a progressive revelation or discovery, revelation is God reaching down: discovery is man reaching up. It must be recognized that the book contains many kinds of writing. There are history, poetry, drama, sermons, letters, folk tales. The books of Jonah and Job are clearly dramatic presentations whose purpose is not to tell you of something that actually happened but to convey spiritual insight or warning. It is no tribute to the Bible to insist that an historical person named Jonah really lived for three days inside a big fish, composing a long prayer while in the fish's belly, or to assert that the long, fascinating conversations between Job and his three friends actually took place. It is, in fact, only when one is liberated from such literalism that one can experience the full power of these books.

It does not enhance the Bible's greatness to insist that the magnificent poem in praise of the Creator and his works in the first and second chapters of Genesis must be read as a factual account of how the world began and how man came into existence. Thanks be to God -- and to the Hebrews -- for an interpretation whose validity and nobility far excel accounts of the world's beginning in Persian and Hindu sacred literature! But the truth of the Genesis story does not depend on the specific details. One God -- not many gods -- who makes man in his own image; that's enough. We can leave the details to science.

. . . . .

In sum, the Bible should be read, neither as always infallible or "divine," nor as "merely human." Both are extremes that serious and intelligent people will avoid. All of the Bible is interesting, except perhaps the Book of *Numbers*. Most of it is important.

Some of it -- the peaks in the great Hebrew prophets and in the life and teachings of Jesus -- is immeasurably important.

(©*The Ledger*, February 12, 1972)

The Bible Says

It has often been observed -- sometimes ruefully, sometimes cynically -- that the Bible can be quoted in support of almost anything one wants to believe or do. Whether or not the Bible actually supports the wide variety of belief and practice to be found among its readers, it is a fact that the book is confidently quoted by people who take different, sometimes irreconcilable, positions.

. . . . .

Name almost any opinion or belief -- religious, moral, political, economic -- and someone will find Biblical support or rejection of it. Conservative and fundamentalist preachers, on the one hand, and liberal preachers, on the other, make extensive use of Bible stories and statements. "Poor Bible," one might say, "How you are pulled in all directions!"

What are we to make of this situation? It won't do for liberals and conservatives to accuse each other of not "sticking to the Bible." The plain fact is people in both groups make constant use of the book. One way of answering the question is to say that most Bible readers do not take their beliefs, especially their beliefs on social questions, from the Bible; their beliefs are formed by the environment in which they live, by their childhood and adult experiences, by their inherited politics and their economic interests; then they find in the Bible stories and statements that back up what they believed before they opened the book.

. . . . .

Observing the wide variety of Bible interpretation and the disputes, sometimes acrimonious, about its meaning, some people say: Let's not bother with the Bible. It says so many different things, and who can say whose interpretation is the right one? In any case, why do we have to go back two or three thousand years for spiritual guidance? Did God stop speaking when the Bible was closed?

It is of course true that wisdom and insight can be found in many other places: in the Koran, in the sayings of Buddha, in the teaching of Gandhi, in the Indian Bhagavad Gita, to take only a few examples. Nevertheless, something enormously important to mankind came into the world with the Hebrew epic and the Christian event. The Judeo-Christian religion is a central element in the life-stream of, at least, the Western world. And the great and important story of its beginnings is told nowhere except in the Bible. It is a towering book whose influence has been, and is, immeasurable.

(©*The Ledger*, February 5, 1972)

Authority of The Bible

More recently, Herman had these thoughts about those who liked to speak of the authority of the Bible:

> For more than a thousand years, authority for Christians was in the Roman Catholic hierarchy headed by the Pope, who was the supreme authority, the vice-regent of Christ. Luther rejected this authority and put in its place the authority of the Scriptures. Later on, Lutheranism entered a time of rigid orthodoxy, orthodoxy being tested not directly by belief in the Bible, but in acceptance of the creeds: Nicene, Apostles, the Augsburg Confession. This was not fundamentalism as we know it today, but it was close to fundamentalism.
>
> Lutheran and Calvinistic orthodoxy were undermined by Schliermacher and others, giving rise to "liberal" Christianity.
>
> Now in the "liberal" United Church of Christ, a movement has begun to restore the "authority" of the Bible, which again, if not fundamentalism, is close to it, even to insisting on "the *physical* resurrection." (My emphasis.)
>
> It is the old human hunger for authority, the authority of the written biblical text being substituted for the authority of the church. We are afraid of freedom, the freedom to judge and weigh, to accept or reject. We must have an authority. Without an authority -- concrete, tangible -- we seem to say, we are lost in spiritual and moral chaos.
>
> "The kings of the Gentiles," said Jesus, "lord it over man . . . but so shall it not be among you." (*Matthew 20:25-26)* Christians have one authority: Jesus as the Christ. The Bible witnesses to this Jesus, but the Bible as written words is not our authority. Understood with the aid of *reliable* historical and biblical witnesses to Christ, but not, word for word, a final authority. Sifting and interpretation is necessary. And this must be done in perfect freedom, without submission to any dogma of biblical authority. As Luther -- no fundamentalist -- insisted, the whole Bible is to be read and tested by its conformity to Christ. The Word of God is not in

printed words, but in Jesus as the Christ. No Christian should hold up a copy of the Bible and say, "This is the word of God." The word of God is in a person, not in a book.

Jesus does not, of course, stand completely alone, by himself. To hear him we must listen to what we call the Old Testament, listen also to what we can learn from the Bible and from other sources about the life of the Jews in Jesus' time, listen also to what Paul and other early Christians added to our understanding of Jesus. But in the printed words there is no finality, no ultimate authority. The Bible is not to be read as slaves might read orders from a master. It is to be read in freedom. As St. Paul said, "For freedom Christ has set us free. Stand fast therefore, and do not submit again to a yoke of slavery." *(Galatians 5:1)*

(Rumination, April 21, 1984)

The Use and Misuse of the Bible

Herman further developed his ideas that the Bible should not be interpreted literally in a sermon "The Use and Misuse of the Bible":

If we do not read the Bible as a series of writings by human beings, who were limited and subject to error and who wrote out of a particular time and for a particular people, we shall never understand the book. But the Bible reaches such depths and heights, is so packed with great insight and great truth, that the last thing one wants to do is to seem to minimize it. You must not therefore take this sermon as a final or adequate word about the Bible, but only as an attempt to say some things that help us to understand the book.

I shall quote here from a useful little book entitled *Modern Man Looks at the Bible*. The writer says, "We are not asked in reading the Bible to believe in serpents and asses that talk, axe heads that float, and suns that stand still. The Biblical writers were not morons. They knew as well as we that these things do not happen. But they were Orientals who were not cursed by having literal Western minds. They told incredible tales. They used poetry, imagery, symbolism, hyperbole. They knew that truth can at times be told only by a myth, and that a legend can sometimes tell us more than a bare fact. What they were concerned with was to make a point of some sort, to teach a moral or religious lesson.

Well, then, someone asks, "How do you in reading the Bible tell what is fact and what is not fact?" There are two answers to this question. First, in reading the Bible, you use your God-given brains. For example: Here is a story about *Joshua*, successor to Moses. Joshua was a general who led the Israelites in great battles. Now listen to this from the 10th chapter of Joshua. "On that day when the Lord delivered the Amorites into the hands of Israel, Joshua spoke with the Lord and said: *Stand still, O Sun in Gideon. Stand still, Moon, in the valley of Aijalon.*" So, the story says, the sun stood still so that the Israelites could take vengeance on their enemies by daylight. That is a powerfully poetic way of saying what a mighty fellow Joshua was. The Hebrews, like modern nations, were always sure God was fighting on their side. You and I know that if the sun stood still the whole solar system would be wrecked. It is not reverence for the Bible but a misuse of it to try to make yourself believe that the sun stood still to help out the Israelites.

I said a few minutes ago that when we read the Bible we should use our God-given minds, our intelligence. But there is a little more to it. Much of the book can be read by anyone, without help -- the marvelous stories told by Jesus, for example, and some of the letters of St. Paul. But for other parts we need the help of men and women who have given their lives to a close study of the book. It is not always easy to put ourselves in the place of people who lived 2800 or 2000 years ago and get the meaning of their words and their experience. The scholars can help us. It is one of the functions of Christian teachers, ministers, Church School leaders and others to help us get behind the words to the people and the situations then existing and then to show how what they learned applies to us. There is eternal truth in the Bible, but the eternal truth was spoken in a time profoundly different from our time. The more we go behind the written words, the more we know about the people and the times in which they wrote, the richer the Bible becomes for us.

Why do so many people want to believe in an infallible book? We must say, I think, that it is a reflection of the human longing for certainty. The same desire for something we can absolutely depend on caused the Roman Catholic cardinals in the year 1870 to declare the Pope infallible when he speaks *ex cathedra,* that is, when he speaks on a matter of faith and morals. One must say that the notion of papal infallibility is a logical development of Biblical infallibility because there is really no point in having an infallible book unless you have an infallible authority to interpret it.

But while our human longing for guidance that is absolutely dependable, something in which there is no error, is understandable, it is nevertheless mistaken. In our time, particularly when so many old beliefs are being shaken, there is an almost frantic clinging to the Bible as the one source of absolute and dependable truth. Some of us ask for concentration on the Bible in our Church School, feeling that if young people are taught the Bible they will have something solid when everything solid seems to liquefy. Granted, this is not an easy time for young people. But if we teach them a view of the Bible that later on they will certainly have to unlearn, we do them more harm than good. Let us teach them, for example, that the Ten Commandments were not written on tables of stone by the finger of God on Mt. Sinai and brought down from the mountain by Moses on a certain day, but that these great rules for living were slowly evolved over long years of trial and tribulation as a wandering tribe of people learned to live together. There is no magic here; there is an interaction between human beings and between human beings and their God. What the spiritually gifted Hebrews learned and bequeathed to us is magnificent and imperishable and well may we say, "It is God's doing and it is marvelous in our eyes." Let us teach young people that the slow development or revelation of one God, instead of many quarrelling gods, was a stupendous achievement, without which, for one thing, modern science would not have been possible. Let us teach them that no matter how much Bible they know, they will never as human beings be free of responsibility to make hard choices.

To teach the Bible is not the purpose of Christian Education. The purpose is to help our young people to use the gift of life in responsible and reverent fashion, to care about their neighbors, to be good stewards of the earth's riches. To know about Moses is no great gain unless we learn something from his experience about how we should live. We study the Bible to learn how God dealt with people long ago in order to learn how he deals with us today.

It's no use to learn about something that happened way back then, unless by learning that we find guidance for ourselves now. As the Bible says, "God is not the God of the dead but of the living."

(Sermon, April 17, 1977)

Caricaturist unknown

Herman had a real zest for life that surfaced in his appreciation of the world and human relations.

Chapter VII. HUMOR AND LIFE

Edited by Katherine Warren, and
Harry and Betty Woodman, parishioners,
First Congregational Church of Greenwich,
Old Greenwich, Connecticut

Herman Reissig was personally dedicated to striving for a better world and a greater appreciation of God through his preaching. As a result, he often became impatient with the frivolous and mundane. Nevertheless, he had a real zest for life that surfaced in his appreciation of the beauty of the world and human relations.

This chapter focuses on Herman as a person rather than as a pastor and prophet, although the three are inextricably entwined.

HUMOR

Herman was an intensely serious individual who loved deep discussions, but did not enjoy "cocktail party" conversation and other trivia. However, he enjoyed good stories and jokes in proper context. He also enjoyed satire and was quite a good satirist himself.

Herman's humor often took the form of satire arising from his frustrations. We can all relate to this parable about committees which appeared in *Christianity and Crisis*, whose editor described Herman as a "church bureaucrat who has, somehow, managed to retain his sense of humor":

> *Minutes of the Meeting of the Hebrew Committee on Relations with Other Nations -- January 6, 800 B.C.*
>
> *Chairman:* Our principal business today is consideration of a draft statement on war and peace by Mr. Isaiah. Since the statement was delivered to you by runners in advance of

this meeting, let us assume that all of us have read it. If there is no objection, we will first have comments on the statement as a whole and then consider it word by word. Are there general comments?

Mr. Benjamin: The statement is too long. The olive growers in our synagogue won't even look at a statement as long as this.

Mr. Judah: In the first paragraph, it says: "They shall beat their spears into pruning hooks and their swords into ploughshares." What about sling shots? Shouldn't they be included?

Chairman: How would you word the addition?

Mr. Judah: Well, the sling shots could be made into children's toys.

Chairman: Will the secretary read what he has down on that?

Secretary: They shall beat their spears into pruning hooks and their swords into ploughshares and the sling shots shall be given to children to play with.

Mr. Jonathan: Third paragraph, line two: "Nation shall not, etc." Are we in a position to make such a positive statement? Making the final decisions is not the function of this committee.

Mr. Jehu: I agree. I suggest the following reading: "In our opinion, nation should not lift up sword against nation or study war any more."

Chairman: All in favor of this change will say "Aye."

Mr. Samuel: Before we vote on that, I feel the lack in this statement of any motivation. Who are we? And why are we saying anything at all on this subject? I don't know quite how to word it but there ought to be something about our basic Hebrew motives and objectives.

Chairman: How about this? "As Hebrews and guardians of the law given at Sinai, it is our opinion, etc."

Mr. Jonathan: That sounds presumptuous. We are not the only Hebrews and guardians of the law. We have no right to speak for everybody.

Mr. Judah: You are probably right. How about this? "As the Committee on Relations with Other Nations, and as one-thousandth of one per cent of the guardians of the law, and speaking only for ourselves, we are on the whole of the opinion, etc."

Mr. Benjamin: I'm not quite satisfied with the reference to pruning hooks. Let's be realistic. If all the spears in the country were turned into pruning hooks, we'd have more pruning hooks than we'd know what to do with.

Mr. Jehu: Mr. Chairman, I move that a sub-committee be appointed to re-draft Mr. Isaiah's statement, taking into account the suggestions made here, and that we meet again after the new moon to consider the revision.

Mr. Eliphaz: I hope the sub-committee will take into consideration that the comma in the third line from the top ought to be a semicolon.

Chairman: Thank you very much, gentlemen. I think we all want to thank Mr. Isaiah for his very fine statement. At our next meeting I hope we can come up with something really good.

(©*Christianity and Crisis, Inc.*, May 11, 1959)

His frustrations about world affairs resulted in this open letter to a newspaper columnist:

A few days ago while waiting for a waitress to bring my lunch, I read in the Boston *Herald* your column reporting a press conference held by Senator Stennis of Mississippi. The Senator had just come home from a trip around the world and he was, according to your column, upset because he thinks Uncle Sam is carrying more than his share of the world's burden. You quote the Senator asking, "How long can we carry this burden? How much can we endure, and for how many years?"

When the waitress brought the food I could hardly eat it. I felt so sorry for myself and all the other poor, overburdened Americans. Big tears splashed down on my meager fare of potato soup and water. The Senator is right! We can't carry this burden much longer. Look at the state we are in already! The highways and city streets have practically no cars left on them. And when you look at the measly little cars that *are* on the road -- well they're hardly better than old worn-out bicycles. The shelves in our supermarkets are almost bare. And Americans aren't drinking much anymore. They can't afford it.

Most of the beauty shops have closed and our women are beginning to look awful. The men you see on the streets are virtually in rags.

The few new office buildings going up around the country are little better than shacks.

I don't know if Senator Stennis is a religious person, but I am and I'd like to take the Senator with me on my travels around the country. When I see the new church buildings being erected in the city suburbs I get boiling mad. These miserable plain wooden structures that hardly keep out the rain! How can we build churches that truly glorify God when we have to give so much money to other people?

I say again: the Senator is right! We must get rid of this crushing burden. Right away!

(Letter, October 26, 1959)

We all have our pet pleasures and peeves. Later in his life, Herman, as was his wont, put his in writing:

My Greatest Pleasures
(not necessarily in order of greatest pleasure)

1. The pleasure (mingled with pain) of trying to get a difficult subject straight in my head and then putting it in words that will bring it alive to a congregation.
2. Preaching in First Church, Old Greenwich.
3. A dinner party with congenial and intelligent friends.
4, Seeing my children and grandchildren.
5. Writing and receiving personal letters.
6. Hugging my wife in bed, etc.
7. Reading a good book.
8. Working in the garden and watching things grow.
9. Bringing garden stuff into the house.
10. Eating my wife's meals.
11. The first swallow of orange juice in the morning.
12. Seeing buds open on bushes and trees in the spring.

My Greatest Aversions
(not necessarily in order of depth of aversion)

1. Making up a king-size bed.
2. Washing windows.
3. Paying $4.50 for a 5-minute haircut.
4. Having my attention drawn to stains on my clothes. (An unreasonable aversion.)
5. Junk mail.
6. Speakers and writers who use incorrect or clumsy English.
7. Advertising on TV.
8. People who spend more on luxury and pleasure than I spend.
9. People who drop trash in public places.
10. People without a sense of humor.
11. Richard Nixon.
12. People who make scapegoats of politicians.

(Rumination, undated)

Christmas letters always extol virtues and good times. Herman apparently took exception in this Rumination:

(*Note*: We are getting many Christmas letters that tell us, *in great detail*, what has happened to our friends in the past year. The greetings we sent out said nothing about what happened to *us*. We are, therefore, despite the extra expense, sending a true historical résumé to at least a few of the people on our list.)

Last summer in Connecticut (Do you know or care that we have a little house there?) our sole TV went on the blink. Not only were we without soap operas and other kinds of high culture for five weeks but in trying to get the thing repaired we had one of the most exasperating consumer experiences that any consumer has ever had. For five weeks we were mad a good part of every day.

Coming back to Lakeland in October, we found our relatively new refrigerator leaking so badly that the freezer section was useless. It took the repair man five days to get here and then three weeks more to come with a replacement for the deceased part. Almost every day Frances was in tears in her effort to prepare her customary high-grade meals, sometimes being compelled to resort to that worst of all American culinary abominations, a "TV dinner." Of course, we had no ice cubes for regular cocktail hour.

Next, one of our two heating systems began shooting in cold, instead of hot, air. The weather being unseasonably cold, Herman could not use his study without unbearable discomfort. And, what with inflation and everything, these breakdowns cost money. Plenty!

Moths ate holes in Herman's favorite pants during the summer and other pants were damaged by sparks from his pipe. About forty of the eighty petunia plants he set out with loving care, died. This just about spoiled the fall for him -- and for Frances also, through having to listen to his moaning. You will be interested to know that he bought, for the first time, two Arcotis plants (African-daisy). Just when one of the pretty blossoms was in full bloom on its long, tender stem, the cat bit it off.

Last summer Frances ordered a number of little kitchen gadgets from a mail order house. The gadgets for poaching eggs turned out to be completely useless. Only today, a can of plastic wood that was needed for work on a new homemade bookcase vanished without a trace. As soon as we got back to Lakeland we began spending some time every day putting together a big, round jigsaw puzzle, the most difficult one we have ever encountered. For thirty minutes at a time we sometimes could not fit in even one new piece, but we couldn't stay away from the damn thing. In the moment of final triumph, one piece was missing! Frances tore out some of her long hair and Herman used the worst language ever heard south of the Mason-Dixon line.

During the first weeks in Connecticut last summer Frances complained of a stuffed-up nose and during August Herman had a slight throat irritation.

We do hope you had a good year.

(Rumination, December 17, 1969)

Most males will empathize with these thoughts of Herman's while wrapping Christmas presents for his wife:

Almost all women wrap Christmas presents with easy artistry. When my wife's gifts are put in my hands on Christmas day, the destruction of the lovely wrapping seems almost sacrilegious. So much art turned so quickly into a litter of paper and string on the floor! It may be that some men do this as well as women.

As for me, one of the Lord's chief means of keeping me humble, not to say despondent, is the contemplation of my personally-wrapped Christmas packages. I go into my study, shut the door, prop a chair against it to keep out intruders, bring out my smuggled-in packages, produce from here and there sheets of gorgeous wrapping paper, scotch tape, colored string, decorative ribbons, a pair of shears. Then begins a task that should be full of secret pleasure but, year after year, is actually a mortification of the spirit.

The pieces of wrapping paper are always too small or too large. However symmetrical the lines of the gift, in my hands it invariably becomes about as easy to wrap as a camel. Prodigal use of scotch tape helps, but not much. One of the triangles, when I bring it over the end of the box, is always larger than its mate at the other end. Should the folded edges be on top or on the bottom? I can never remember. Sometimes they are on top and look quite unbeautiful; sometimes they are on the bottom and look equally unattractive. As for tying bows with the lovely wide ribbon -- how *does* one make them come out even and unwrinkled?

Well, the job is done. I carry my packages to the tree where, as I look at them lying next to my wife's exquisite work, they almost take the joy out of Christmas. It doesn't help much to know that, being a woman of great forbearance, she will surely say to herself, "Oh well! At least the man tried."

Last year as the labor was proceeding about as usual, or perhaps a little worse -- since age increaseth not my wrapping skill -- I began to wonder about other men. Some of them I have met, others are only names and faces I have seen in newspapers. It seemed to me that if I could see them wrapping presents for their wives I would know them with a knowledge that could be gained in no other way. The fact is, I have never seen any other man in the act of wrapping presents. This is a great loss. How can I know the real Lyndon Baines Johnson if I can't visualize him wrapping his presents for Lady Bird? How do Dean Rusk's packages look? And Governor Romney's? In what room in his house in Independence, Mo., and with what inelegant exclamations does Harry Truman wrap a bottle of cologne for Bess?

Don't tell me all these people are bright, capable, wonderful husbands and fathers -- that sort of superficial stuff! Let's go deeper! Just how good are they at wrapping Christmas packages?

As an afterthought, it occurs to me that some men here may be too lazy or too cowardly even to try doing the wrapping themselves. They let the store do it for them!

Concerning such a man, I can only say: May God have mercy on his soul!

(Rumination, undated)

Herman frequently wrote letters to the editor. In this one, he sardonically expressed his envy of the owner of a $125,000 car:

I missed your news story on the $125,000 car being built in Stamford, but I read your March 12 editorial, and your description of the car fills me with a resolution: I am not exactly wealthy, but I must have one of those cars.

Having acquired the car, I visualize myself doing things that will make me feel really good. First, I shall buy a personal wardrobe to go with the car; a handsomely-tailored suit, silk shirt, and all the rest. Then I shall get in the car -- but wait a minute; I shall want a chauffeur so that I will be free to look down on the people I pass. My driver will be directed to pass the Salvation Army headquarters where I shall hope to see a line of hungry people lined up in expectation of some food. We will drive very slowly so that the hungry can see me and I will have a chance to savor my satisfaction at not being like them.

Next, we will drive to the Bronx, past rotting tenements, hoping to see some families being evicted. This will make me thankful for my comfortable home. If I hear of 25 jobs being advertised, I shall drive there past the 1,000 people lined up to apply for a job and let them admire me and my car. If I am inclined to go to church, I shall first enquire if the minister is properly respectful toward owners of $125,000 cars. I want none of this mushy, socialistic stuff about "compassion." When my ego has been sufficiently inflated by the envy of "those less fortunate than I," I shall drive to Washington and circle the White House until President Reagan, if he is not vacationing on his ranch or in the Bahamas, notices me. My expectation is that if he sees me in my car he will say, "There's the kind of man I want in my administration! Bring him in and give him a desk right next to the Oval Office."

I urge all others who can somehow scrape together $125,000 to buy one of these cars. Let us not, like the editorial writer, confine ourselves to wishing the car manufacturers well.

There is only one small catch in this plan of mine. Historians of American life are just about unanimous in their lack of admiration for the very rich of our recent past because of what is called their "conspicuous consumption." Would my grandchildren despise, instead of admire, me? Also, I made the mistake recently of re-reading Charles Dickens' novel, *A Tale of Two Cities*. In this story of the French revolution of 1789, Dickens describes the beastly ferocity of the poor, who brought their knitting to the guillotine and gleefully watched members of the aristocracy being beheaded. But Dickens -- confound the man! -- keeps reminding us that the awful violence of the masses was the direct fruit of the heartless indifference of the aristocracy. Would I be able to ride in my car without remembering such things?

Further, there is that story in the Bible that, in spite of my best efforts to forget it, I keep remembering. It is the story of a "rich man who fared sumptuously every day" while a poor man at his feet would have been glad for a few crumbs from his table. The Bible in its picturesque way says the rich man went to hell while the poor man rested comfortably on Abraham's bosom. I read that story when I was young, although I don't remember hearing it read in any church in a long time.

Mr. Editor, I must end by confessing to being a little less sure about wanting that car. Do you think I should settle for a Rolls Royce?

(Letter, March 23, 1982)

Herman's thoughts on a news story from Hollywood after reading Reinhold Niebuhr's latest book triggered this bit of satire in his earlier years:

The dialectical relationship between the sentimental Sinatra and the prideful Ava Gardner has not produced even the provisional harmony of interests which is all that we have a right to expect within the confines of man's historical existence. The present ambiguous position of these two products of our rather fatuous liberal culture provides another illustration of the nemesis which always overtakes the pride of man and the pretensions of women. Suffering from utopian illusions, and with their thinking insufficiently informed by the profound insights of Kierkegaard, Frank and Ava have not been aware of the contingent character of even the loftiest human ideals. The inconclusive debate between them has failed to resolve their antinomies or to impose coherence upon incoherence. Once again the vitalities of human life have been demonstrated to be beyond the capacity of the rational mind to control. Paradoxically, their quasi-relationship was both good and evil. It was good because it arose from natural desires which are insufficiently appreciated in the Platonic tradition. It was evil because their self-idolatry was in radical contradiction to the fact of man's creatureliness. There is a rough justice in the sad reduction of their inordinate hopes to "ordinancy." Incidentally, the error in Sinatraism, which betrays some traces of Rousseauism, lies in the ascription of an absolute validity to his emotional attachment to the particularity called Ava, whereas the truth of the matter is that without the presupposition of Ava's indispensability to his happiness, and with a less consistent pursuit of the finite object, a closer approximation to a tolerable harmony might actually be achieved. Thus their failure is both evidence of the tragic character of human existence and the vindication of the prophetic judgment that "the heathen have raged and the people of Hollywood have imagined a vain thing."

(Rumination, December 2, 1953)

We conclude this section with Herman's contemporary form of a parable:

Three men went to church to pray, the first a politician, the second a preacher and the third a businessman. The politician bowed his head and prayed, "God, I thank you that

I am not like other men, each serving his own private interest, or even as this preacher and this businessman. I wrestle daily with great issues of public welfare. I serve the public. I am a part of the high and necessary function of government."

The preacher knelt and said, "God, I thank you that I am engaged in a sacred calling. I work, not for profit, but for the good of my people. I deal with the only finally important things. I stand for faith, hope, and love."

The businessman lifted his eyes to heaven and prayed, "God, I thank you that I am not a politician who spends other people's money, who compromises, wheels and deals and thinks only of the next election, or even as this preacher who speaks lofty, impractical ideals. I work hard and efficiently. I help to create the wealth on which all others depend. God, I thank you that I am a businessman."

I say to you that none of these three went home justified before God, for he who exalts himself and demeans others commits the sin of phariseeism. Only he who recognizes and confesses his own sin is acceptable to the God of justice and mercy.

(Rumination, May, 1981)

LIFE

This section presents some of Herman Reissig's words on four important life topics -- marriage, sexuality, retirement and death.

Marriage

In one of his ruminations after the death of his wife of many years, Frances (known affectionately as Bun), he considered the desirability of remarrying:

> Possible? Of course. Desirable? My soul longeth, yea even fainteth for a permanent woman companion. What kind of woman, at seventy-five, do I look for?
>
> One with whom, if I were passionately in love with the sea, I would be willing to cross the Atlantic in a rowboat.
>
> One with whom I could happily sit at home through an evening and talk or not talk.
>
> One with whom I would be glad to go for a long walk on city streets or in the woods.
>
> One who can laugh at herself -- and at me.
>
> One who has a sense of her own worth, accepts herself, but is neither conceited nor badly self-centered.
>
> One who is religious but not pious, spiritual but not addicted to religious formalities.
>
> One who likes to be with people but also can be alone.
>
> One who is fascinated by the endless variety of life, who does not automatically turn away from "bad" people, is open to new experiences.
>
> One who likes lovely things (furniture, art) but can feel at home in simple surroundings; one who likes good food but can be happy "when we on simple rations sup."
>
> One who cares more for reality than for "appearance."
>
> One who, if the specific sex drive is no longer so urgent, still wants to be caressed and to caress, for whom arms around and kisses in bed are a delightful way of expressing love. "Nor spirit helps flesh more than flesh helps spirit."
>
> (Rumination, February, 1974)

In his "Comments" at the marriage ceremony of good friends, Herman explores the institution of marriage:

Love between a man and woman, it is maintained, can be real and durable without marriage and we know marriage can exist (though it cannot thrive) without love. Which is to say that marriage may not always be indispensable to love but love is always indispensable to marriage. Men and women, we may be sure, will always be drawn to each other by that exciting mixture of feelings we call love. Some now say that such love can thrive without marriage. This theory has yet to be tested in the laboratory of human experience. It may turn out that without marriage love cannot make its full contribution to individuals or to society.

For what is love? It is the capacity for caring simultaneously for one's self and for another self. And the propinquity and special intimacy of marriage make it the supreme test of our capacity for doing this. How to be one's self, to be true to one's own genius, to bring the unique personal bud to its fullest possible flowering, but not to hurt or suppress, but to help another self -- that is the challenge of marriage. Which means that marriage requires toughness and patience, intelligence and genuine caring. In every sphere, but especially in marriage, it is not enough to do one's own thing,for doing one's own thing may mean the denial of love.

Marriage sets a social seal upon love, but the institution carries with it no guarantee that the love that led to it will grow and be enduring. Marriage is a gamble for high stakes. If the gamblers lose, the loss is painful. If they win, the gain is very sweet. And the gain is not only to the marriage partners; it is a gain for society and particularly for those who know the married pair. To think about the marriage of a man and a woman and to be able to say that it is good is a strong moral tonic.

Wherefore you are now adjured, by one who loves you and who also cares for the well-being of all persons, to use every resource of mind and heart to make this a good marriage. You did not have to marry, even though you have been in love with each other. But having decided upon marriage, you cannot without some loss to yourselves and to others, fail to make it good. This is not to say that you *must* stay together until the mortal thread is broken. You are not now chained together by the marriage ceremony; you are liberated into a lovely and noble enterprise. And this enterprise is worth all the intelligence, toughness, patience and moral concern you can muster.

Because we are not gods but human beings struggling toward a truer personhood, no marriage can be without tension. If there is no tension in the marriage, one of two conditions is present: either man and wife have ceased to care or one of them has surrendered his integrity by good constitutional provisions and by goodwill, but also by the operation of what we call countervailing forces -- forces as nearly equal as possible, which confront one another, assert, demand, compromise, give. Just so in marriage. A good marriage is produced, not only by a steady yearning toward each other, but also by two forces, not too unequal, that assert, confront, adjust and give.

(Marriage Service, date unknown)

Herman united religious traditions in another marriage service:

You come from different religious traditions, one Jewish, the other Christian. In uniting the two religions in your married life, you bring together what never should have been separate. You now have a chance to demonstrate, as others have demonstrated, that loyalty to one's own religion, respect for its traditions, and love for its people can be combined with reverence for another religion. It is an honor and a deeply moving privilege for me, a Christian minister whose living roots are in the Jewish faith, to unite in marriage a Jewish man and a Christian woman.

You are both children of God, the God in whom all of us live and move and have our being. The name of God speaks to all of us, saying "You shall love the Lord your God with all your heart and mind and soul and your neighbor as yourself."

Both of you love the world of nature, all living and growing things. It is through love of our fellow men and through reverence for all created things that we love and honor God. Here among the trees we may hear an ancient Hebrew poet say "The trees of the wood shall clap their hands and all the sons of God shall sing for joy."

The members of your families and your friends pray that your married life will be such that the trees of the wood will indeed clap their hands and all who know you sing for joy. If there be in your minds any question about your religious obligations, I remind you of the words of a great Hebrew prophet: "What does the Lord require of you but to do justice and to love mercy and to walk humbly with your God?"

(Marriage Service, October 4, 1969)

In this rumination about his marriage to Florence, Herman comments amusingly about the need for some diversity (but not too much) in marriage:

At dinner last night I said to Flo, "I want to ask you a question: Do you think our relationship is characterized by complementarity?" With her usual perspicacity, she replied that she thought there was a fairly high degree of asymmetrical complementarity. This, it seems to me, is the way it should be. If the complementarity is always symmetrical, one might as well be married to one's self, for one always agrees with one's own opinions and there is thus none of the argumentation that makes life interesting. If, on the other hand, the asymmetry is too constant and acute, the relationship may become a laceration of the spirit.

In our case, when the asymmetry threatens the disintegration of marital harmony, we talk about the weather, concerning which we can always lovingly agree that it is either too hot or too cold. Or we converse about Ronald Reagan, on whom we can with beautiful concord concur that he is a disaster.

When Flo feels our symmetrical tranquillity is getting a bit sticky, she calls my attention to a grease spot on my jacket. This always leads to violent argument, I insisting that it doesn't matter enough to justify her in disturbing my profound theological reflections, and she insisting that the spot must immediately be removed.

In this way, alternating between symmetry and asymmetry, we have managed for nine years to stay together.

(Rumination, January 11, 1983)

Herman's imaginative analogy in his sermon "Ultimate Goals and Present Opportunities" provides yet another approach to married life:

Consider marriage. No use dreaming about an absolutely perfect relationship: there are none. Two persons living together day after day, year after year, each keeping his or her own sense of personal identity and worth, yet achieving a union of trust and mutual support; that, when you stop to think about it, is some achievement! And how is it accomplished? If, when the inevitable tensions and annoyances come, the married person concentrates on ideal visions, saying, "O, I wish, I wish," well, then you're sunk. Dealing with a married partner is something like dealing with your automobiles. If one of the spark plugs stops firing, you don't necessarily have to rush off to buy a new car. You do something simple about it -- right now. Given a reasonable degree of goodness in each of the two persons, the key to building a good relationship is in little actions and small changes that you can take today. Don't sit there dreaming how wonderful it would be if. . . . say something or do something good now.

(Sermon, August 8, 1976)

In his sermon "That Marriage May Be What Marriage Can Be," Herman suggested a time to reflect: (Note that he has recognized the need to use inclusive language in spite of still being uncomfortable with it.)

Let me suggest a simple, practical way to encourage the mutual respect and regard that is the true basis of a good

> marriage. Suppose both are sitting in the living room, reading a book or newspaper. Put down what you are reading and quietly look at that man or woman sitting there. Just look and think. There he, or she, is -- a person, a being of worth, even infinite worth. Before that person belongs to you, he, she belongs to himself, to God, has his or her own destiny. (This "he" or "she" business is a nuisance.) Thinking like that you may tremble a little inside. How astonishing that you are together at all! If there has been trouble, discontent, try getting down to a deeper level. Tell your egotism to go away for a minute. You might even imagine to yourself how God thinks about the person sitting there. It could be that as you look and think, you will find love and desire for closer contact welling up in you, want to get as close as two human beings can get. Or the thinking might make you decide to be more thoughtful and helpful than you have been. Do you ever think calmly and as objectively as possible about your husband or wife?
>
> (Sermon, date unknown)

Sexuality

Herman was not timid about introducing sexuality in his preachings and writings:

> Next Sunday I officiate at the marriage of a man 79 and a woman 78. They wanted me, perhaps thinking *I* would have more understanding of marriage in the late years. In yesterday's conference with them I refrained from giving them advice on sex, though I would not be surprised if after long years of widowhood and widowerhood, the juices might start to run again. I suppose that nowadays men and women understand that libido does not die when we get older. I, when young, thought it ended in middle age or before. Fact is, it only becomes somewhat less insistent and demanding. My brother told me, in a rare moment of confidence, "I functioned until I was eighty." Let this be a reminder to you: as long as there is life, there is hope! (Is such talk the result of reading Driver?) One reason for wishing I could begin my life over again: I could grow to adulthood with a clean

concept of sex. How hardly does one recover from the ugly, secretive ideas of youth-as-it-used-to-be!

(Letter, June 8, 1978)

In a sermon, "Christian Permissiveness," Herman suggested a balance between sexual suppression and permissiveness:

A strain of denial and rejection of sex entered Christian teaching in the religion's early days, coming not from the Hebrews (the strict Pharisees called Jesus "a glutton and a drinker") but from Persian and other sources. Ever since in the Western world, we have swung back and forth between trying to push the sensual out of sight and letting go without restraint. The Elizabethan Age of openness was followed by the Victorian Age of repression. With probably some unfairness to our Puritan forefathers, we identify treating sex as a guilty secret with Puritanism. We now face a double danger. The first danger is that government supported by powerful sections of the public reacting to unlimited permissiveness will demand and enforce discipline. Freedom would then be interpreted to mean freedom to do what is "right." This used to be how the Roman Catholic hierarchy interpreted freedom, and of course it meant that the hierarchy would decide what is right. About the only places where this kind of disciplined living is now enforced is in fascist and communist countries. We had thought it was communism that would do away with sexual strictness and destroy the family, but now communist regimes absolutely forbid what so-called Christian countries permit. We would better think long and hard before we join another explosion. The idea of tender, protected women, on the one side, and a John Wayne type of man, on the other, does not give us wisdom for the future.

The other danger, and it is a real danger, is that an all-is-permitted attitude could shatter the emotional life of individuals and make a mess of society. We cannot expect those who are making money from permissiveness to care what happens. Their god is money and their appeal to fundamental freedoms in defense of their business is the purest kind of hypocrisy. But those who definitely do not want to return to old ways and are merely happy about freedom without sexual restraint are also wrong. We have not yet found a satisfactory way to handle sex. Neither those who shout "Hurrah" for unlimited permissiveness nor those who want to go back to the old ways can help us. We are dealing here with a drive in human beings that can be even more powerful than hunger for food, a drive that can produce joy and fuller life, but that can also push aside every other need and make miserable slaves of us, as more than one has discovered. If there is too much repression, life becomes joyless and arid. If there is no restraint, the river becomes a swamp.

Without discipline there is no true freedom anywhere. A great organist is magnificently great at the organ because he has subjected himself to the discipline of the organ.

But, to say it again, the old rules cannot be and should not be reinstated. The physical body is not the source of evil and the spirit the source of good. The sexual relation is not, inherently, sinful, evil, wrong, whether it occurs inside or outside marriage. Both the old suppressionism and the new permissiveness reduce sex, the one by surrounding it with shame and guilt and the other by pretending that the explicit sexual act is no more important than smoking a cigarette or taking a drink; the one by isolating sex to half-guilty secrecy and the other by exposing it, as it were, on a store counter. The new restraints must grow out of a new conception of the human being, of nature and spirit, of man and woman, of the interaction of sensual and spiritual. It is this goal that, with much pain and much error, we are struggling toward.

(Sermon, April 8, 1973)

In a sermon, "Jesus, the Human Face of God," Herman discussed Jesus' own sexuality:

Perhaps the best way to get the complete humanity of Jesus into our thinking about him is to talk about the sex instinct. If we cannot risk that, we don't see him as human. If he did not have sexual desires he was a plaster saint. We do not know specifically about that part of his life, the records being understandably silent. But it is not wrong to speculate and guess, as the composer of "Jesus Christ Superstar" and others have done. Moral virtue does not mean not having sexual fantasies and desires. "Purity" does not mean an ethereal kind of living. Indeed, it is a question whether there can be moral or spiritual power in human beings where there is no sexual drive. I believe, I hope, Jesus had some trouble at that point. How could he be my friend or savior without it?

(Sermon, December 19, 1976)

In his column "Something to Think About," Herman commented on Biblical conflicts about sexuality:

The Song of Solomon is a poem in celebration of sensual love. A man sings to his beloved, "Your lips are like a scarlet thread, and your mouth is lovely . . . your two breasts are like two fawns, twins of a gazelle, that feed among the lilies." This is a far cry from New Testament passages that, to put it mildly, take a very severe attitude toward sex. Which of these gives us "the infallible word of God?" The answer must be that the author of the Song of Solomon expresses the Hebrew acceptance of the body as something good and that the asceticism of some New Testament writers was a natural reaction of morally serious people to the licentiousness of the time.

(©*The Ledger*, February 12, 1972)

Herman discussed the human mixture of the physical and spiritual in a sermon "That Marriage May Be What Marriage Can Be":

Something ought to be said about the sex relation. Surely, there is no incompatibility between worship in church and sexual love, even if this is not the place for clinical details. The current flood of books telling men and women how to make love is an inevitable and necessary reaction against the ignorance and sense of shame that have done untold damage. I could tell you about more than one couple who near ruined their own lives and the lives of their children because of sheer ignorance. But reactions always go too far. The philosophy of *Playboy* magazine seems to say, "Let's be like animals." But it is precisely the meaning of human love that it means more than it can mean to animals. The emphasis on techniques in love-making tends to leave out what it is that makes us more than animals.

Many serious writers have tried to describe the specifically human mixture of the physical and the spiritual in sex. They never succeed. I shall not succeed, but let me try to approach the wonderful mystery. The lovers open themselves to each other, without reserve or embarrassment, and certainly without the slightest feeling of shame. They are utterly together in the giving and the receiving, the mutual reaching out, in words and actions. The giving and the receiving is physical. But the physical is then transmuted into a spiritual unity that is inexpressible. The poet Robert Browning put it succinctly in two lines:

Nor soul helps body more now
Than body helps soul.

(Sermon, date unknown)

Retirement

Herman never really retired, or wanted to retire, as he expressed in the following:

A man, on being introduced to me, said, "I understand you are living in retirement." Yes, in some ways one is retired. Retired from clockwatching, from commuting, from the tyranny of the datebook, from a hundred committee meetings, from running, or helping to run, a business or institution, from, what is called, "making a living." But these are the externals of human life. They have their worth and importance; they are not the main business. From the main business of living one need not, should not, retire -- ever. Speaking for myself, I put it like this:

I do not want to be, nor ever need be, retired from studying the world around me and particularly, human history. Seeing myself and my time as a tiny fragment of the long, long sweep of life: from looking out over our planet, its Africa, Asia, Europe, South America, the United States, pondering the sameness and the differences, fascinated, sometimes depressed, by what goes on, weeping with those who weep and rejoicing with those who rejoice. Not retired from considering the truly remarkable history of my own country or its present achievements and corruptions; from contemplating the part of our world called Greenwich -- its special character, its goodness and its weakness, its helpfulness and its dangers to the spiritual life; never ceasing to yearn and learn; never retired from trying to live like a human being, not like a bee that mindlessly performs its functions without tension or creativity; not retired from being a part of the life around me, sharing its victories and its defeats, its aspirations and its weaknesses; continuing to welcome each additional fragment of understanding, without ever supposing that one has arrived at final truth, aware that we know in part and prophesy in part; seeing the relativity of all our knowledge but clinging to some center of commitment that saves from bewilderment and drift; standing in awe before the tremendous story of life in this vast universe; and, most of all, never retired from the task of trying to respect and love my fellow travelers, beginning with those nearest me.

(Rumination, undated)

The call to become Associate Interim Pastor at the First Congregational Church "rescued" Herman from semi-retirement in Florida as he expressed in this excerpt from a column he wrote for *The Ledger,* Lakeland, Florida and which was reprinted in the Old Greenwich paper on November 9, 1972:

The debate with myself about making this radical change came to an end in this fashion:

I: "No, I won't do it. I'm used to the Lakeland routine: lots of leisure, some writing and speaking, visits with dear friends. Why should I return to a scheduled and busy life, if only temporarily?"

ME: "So you are getting old, are you? No zest anymore for something new. Don't want to get out of your pleasant rut. Maybe a little afraid you won't measure up to the job."

That second voice from the inside did the trick. We are in for it now. For both of us, a new home, new friends, quite different kind of weather. For me, many hospital visits, since in a large church some members are always there, meeting with the other eight or ten persons on the church staff, occasional preaching, planning of adult education.

Have we not all read that the way to keep from getting old is to do something involved with some new aspect of human life? This invitation, then, was a test of resiliency and courage. Someone said that retirement is a process of "growing gracefully irrelevant." Bah! Who wants to be irrelevant? Life is too interesting to stand on the sidelines. So the decision was: "Let's go!"

So here we are in Old Greenwich, Connecticut. This is being written four days after our arrival. The house looks almost as if we have lived here for years. New friends come and go, exerting themselves to help the newcomers. On Sunday I assisted in two services, on Monday went to the bank, post office, newspaper office and explored the many rooms of the church, and on Tuesday, I joined a long discussion with the rest of the staff, went to the hospital to make some calls, and asked about getting snow tires for the car. It's exhilarating. I'm shocked to think that listening to the voice of timidity and ease might have deprived us of all this.

It's an old saying that the difference between a rut and a grave is only a question of depth. How easily we slip into ruts! Even young people do it. With middle-age, we become "set" in our ways. Something is right if it's what we are used to; something is wrong if it is unaccustomed. A new idea is rejected out-of-hand; it isn't what we have always done. We want our preachers and politicians to confirm us in what we already believe. Out with innovators! This, of course, spells stagnation.

When Woodrow Wilson was president of Princeton University he introduced needed reforms. The university trustees battled him every inch of the way. Answering them, Wilson said that life is like a plant. Insist on keeping a plant the way it is and it will die. Schools, churches, governments, businesses change or they cease to serve us.

Be careful how you reject an invitation to think a new thought or do something you have never done before. You could be turning your back on life.

(©*The Ledger*, October 28, 1972)

In a rumination, Herman put some thoughts about his retirement in rhyme:

Because I'm no longer dependent on salary,
I'm not so inclined to play up to the gallery.
Instead I now find, getting older and older,
The words that I preach come out bolder and bolder.

(Rumination, May, 1978)

Death

Herman somehow found words to ease the pain of death in a letter to a friend:

Coming back to the apartment from a short walk, I ran into an elderly couple. I said I had just received a sad letter. In a moment the man said, "I know. I lost two of my three sons."

We human beings comfort each other as best we can. As for philosophy, I say to myself and have said to others, human life is *wonderful* and *vulnerable*. Truly wonderful and tragically vulnerable. Courage and faith consist in not losing sight of the wonder when someone close to us gives an example of the vulnerability. I said to the man mentioned above, "I have two sons and if one of them should precede me to the grave I don't see how I could stand it." He said, "But you would!" Yes. And you and your brother and the whole family, being cast down, will go on making the best you can of the unbelievably wonderful gift of life.

Lincoln died at the moment of triumph. Jesus died at thirty-three. Is the gift worth the price? I think so. At any rate, I for one want to see if I can enrich life just a tiny bit, accepting the heartbreaks and their tears, not giving up.

I spent last evening with a man whose wife died suddenly in December. I worked with the woman for years and loved her. Together we listened to a tape of her memorial service. He prepared the supper for the two of us. We even laughed a little before the evening was over.

All this may be some of the meaning of "Our God, Our Help in Ages Past."

In a similar fashion, he wrote this letter of consolation:

On arriving home yesterday we learned that a very dear friend of yours died suddenly. Flo and I are very sorry that my work in the White Plains church is going to make it difficult to see you. But you should know, at least by letter, that we are deeply sorry about your loss. You are the kind of person to whom personal relations mean much. You are feeling, sometimes a sharp stab and sometimes a dull pain. At such times we don't quite believe that the grace of God and the graces of other friendships and of our work are enough. But, knowing you, I know you will find strength and joy for living. You are an inspiration to many of us, not only, or even chiefly, because of what you put into our living, but because of the quality of your spirit. I have counted it one of the main gifts of my association with First Church to have you as a friend . . . I have always liked, particularly, one sentence in the communion service in the Book of Common Prayer: "Lift up your hearts." Lift up your heart, and give thanks that you have been given enough to make so many thankful for you.

Photographer unknown

"Nations do not fight because they have guns; they have guns because they are afraid or because they want what they cannot get without fighting."

Chapter VIII. POLITICS AND WORLD AFFAIRS

Edited by Derek Boothby,
Principal Officer, United Nations, and parishioner,
First Congregational Church of Greenwich,
Old Greenwich, Connecticut

From 1948 to 1965, Herman Reissig was Secretary for International Relations of the Congregational Christian Church's Council for Social Action and of the successor Council for Christian Social Action. Without doubt, he was the man for the job. Widely travelled, with perceptive eye, sharp intellect, vigorous social conscience and unabashed integrity, he addressed a broad range of political and international issues with challenging directness.

Activities

In one of his regular reports on his work, he gave the following list of his activities during the seven-month period of January-July 1958:

- A letter to all churches
- Two special bulletins to social action leaders
- Published articles as follows: two in *Christian Community,* two in *Advance*, two in *The Messenger*, one in *Social Action*
- Testimony on foreign aid before the House and Senate Committees
- Telegram to the House Appropriations Committee
- Travel as follows:
  Number of cities visited - 33
  Number of meetings - 39
  Number of addresses - 54
  Radio interviews - 2
  Television broadcasts - 2

- Recruitment of a special corps of 26 speakers on aid and trade, some of whom made frequent addresses
- Assistance to the Department of International Affairs of the National Council of Churches in preparation of material on aid and trade
- Attendance at the National Conference on Foreign Aid held in Washington, called at the request of the President
- An article in the June issue of *Advance*, dealing mainly with the problem of atomic weapons
- Participation in the Florida, California, Wisconsin and Oberlin Social Action Institutes
- Addresses at the following colleges: Talladega (2), Dillard (1), Wagner (2), Southern University (1)
- Participation in the conference "The Churchman as a Citizen" in Collegeville, Pennsylvania
- One day of speaking for the Florida Chain of Missions
- Leadership of a seminar at the annual meeting of the New York Congregational Conference
- Leadership of the Washington/Idaho Ministers' Retreat
- Chairmanship of the Committee on Education and Action, Department of International Affairs, National Council of Churches (two meetings)
- Participation in a panel at a Church Peace Union seminar
- Between January 1st and July 31st, visits to 19 states, while being in New York on 40 of the 212 days

International Relations

In another report in early 1959, he offered his observations and conclusions at the end of ten years on the CSA and CCSA staff as a specialist in international relations:

1. Most people, especially in the churches, are interested in world affairs, and respond well to our analysis and recommendations *if* the situation and recommendations are clearly presented to them.
2. In only a small fraction of our churches are world affairs taken seriously. The purported "indifference" of members of the churches is, mainly, a reflection of poorly-informed and unimaginative leadership.

3. A vast amount of Christian goodwill and desire for peace goes to waste. It goes to waste because it remains in the realm either of vague criticism or of demand for impossibly perfectionist policies. With respect to the world situation, a useful slogan for local churches would be, "Let's stop moaning and get to work."
4. The contemporary world situation is complicated beyond our power to describe or understand, and no panaceas exist, except in the minds of the poorly-informed. We can see the demands of love and justice in many specific situations but the shape of tomorrow's world cannot be foreseen by human mind or determined by deliberate human action.
5. We can get little sustenance for our efforts in this area from the assurance of contemporary victory. We can be sustained by our belief in the rightness of specific actions, by simple loyalty, and by the faith that, ultimately, "there's a destiny that shapes our ends, rough hew them how we will."
6. A few things are now much more clear than they were a few years ago. And, with respect to these things, it is not too difficult to identify the necessary practical actions:
   a) The whole world is an interdependent neighborhood, so inter-related that almost every action has an almost appalling number of relations and effects. This means that national sovereignty, policies, and actions must increasingly be subsumed under world outlook and planning on a world scale.
   b) The center of power moves away from the West toward the East. We are at the beginning of the end of Western dominance.
   c) Concentration of great wealth in a few areas, with crippling poverty elsewhere, is becoming politically and economically intolerable. On the United States rests a responsibility, in this area, far greater than it has yet assumed.
   d) Communist social orders will not be abolished by denunciation or ostracism or blockade or war. They have evil aspects against which we must struggle.

But if they are not the wave of the future, neither are they the flash floods of a season. Our response should be the dialectical response of criticism-resistance and of appreciation-acceptance.

e) The growing inter-relatedness of human life, coupled with the new forms of power, means that one of two things must happen: either democracy must be able to count on a far more responsible and intelligent participation by individuals, or it must give way to more centralized controls; that is to say, freedom-independence must become more responsible or submit to more limitations.

From the vantage point of 1991 (the year this compendium of Herman Reissig's writings was put together), it might be said that his conclusions have not completely been borne out by events, but such a judgment would be made with the benefit of 30 years of hindsight. What is far more noteworthy is the great extent to which his incisive thoughts and challenging words remain true and fresh today as the day they were written.

The remainder of this chapter includes several illustrations of his writings on public policy issues:

Politics and the Presidency

During the months of 1960, with the eyes of the public turning increasingly to the prospects of a Presidential election that was eventually to place John F. Kennedy in the White House, Herman Reissig addressed "An Open Letter to the Presidential Candidates," published in the *United Church Herald*:

Dear Democratic and Republican Candidates:

From now until next November you will be talking almost constantly to the American people. If one can judge by the past national political contests some of the talk is going to be honest, sensible, enlightening, but much of it will be based on the assumption that the majority of us are childish, ignorant and incorrigibly selfish. Newspaper columnist Roscoe Drummond says we are going to listen to "almost uninterrupted political eyewash."

Crucial Years

For the sake of our country's and the world's well-being, I beg you not to give us eyewash. It might or might not help you win the election; it will certainly do damage to the cause of peace and freedom. Paul G. Hoffman says that, with respect to freedom and economic progress in the undeveloped countries, the next ten years will be crucial. In other areas also the decade ahead will be unusually important. That is why we must have campaign discussions that deal honestly with real issues. Let me be specific.

I hope you will not tell us how "good we Americans have it" and promise that your party will give us more of the same. This is not what Americans ought to be thinking about. Not in this kind of world! It is downright immoral to encourage an individual or a nation to brag about wealth and to think that the most important thing in life is to have more and more of it.

A candidate for high public office has the solemn responsibility not to cater to our immaturity and softness, but to summon us to some show of moral greatness. Our schools, hospitals and other public services are not in good shape. The condition of much housing in our cities is a scandal. The passion for private consumption has dangerously outdistanced our concern for the public good. Please dare to challenge us on these matters.

You will be doing the nation a great service if you explain why no administration can, at this point in history, give the United States a brand new foreign policy. We do need some changes of emphasis and some new ideas. But Republicans did not, despite their promises, change the main items in our response to the world situation, and Democrats, if they should capture the White House in the November election, will not basically revamp United States foreign policy.

This is because a nation that had not entirely lost its good sense was compelled to react to the international situation with such things as foreign aid, increased military power, cultural exchange and removal of at least some restriction on international trade. If Republicans pretend that Communist gains are the fault of President Truman and Secretary of State

Acheson, they falsify the international picture. If Democrats talk as if everything would speedily be better if they were returned to power, they make it extremely difficult for us to get ready for the long, hard pull that is certainly ahead of us and for the kind of resolute and creative actions required of us. Please do not set peace and freedom back in order to set your party ahead!

Tax Money

Talk to us with complete frankness about taxes! We must certainly try to reach international agreements that will lower the fantastic expense of the arms race. But even in this part of the Federal budget it could be that we need to spend more on conventional arms than we are now spending. There must be somewhere in our world a focus of military power, since we have no international system of laws, courts and police power. Do not give the people false expectations of a military budget whittled down to the vanishing point.

As for our other expenses, we need more tax money -- not less -- for world economic development, education, health, housing. Those of us who yearn to keep a larger share of our individual incomes for private use do not understand the nature of industrialized, urbanized society, in which there are more and more needs that cannot be met without public or governmental action. Ever since Franklin D. Roosevelt in 1933 promised to cut Federal expenses, we have had in every campaign a lot of talk about economizing. But every year the budget is larger. It has to be. Not only do we grow richer as a nation, but our public needs increase. Talk to us about the wise use of our wealth, not about keeping more of it for piling up personal possessions.

Better Instincts

Finally, do not insult our intelligence by claiming that your party and only your party can save peace, prosperity and freedom. To be sure, you must criticize current policies and suggest improvements. But if you paint the other party black and yours white, you deceive some people and make the rest more cynical about politicians than they already are. Tell us what needs to be strengthened and what needs to be changed. Talk little about what the other fellows haven't done or wouldn't do. Talk much about what you would do.

In the long run, hardly anything can hurt the United States more than a campaign of "almost uninterrupted political eyewash." If you appeal to the better instincts and the intelligence of the American people you will deserve your country's gratitude. And -- who knows? -- this might be the surest way to get elected.

(©*United Church Herald*, May 12, 1960)

Change Without War

In October 1962, Herman wrote an article published in the magazine *Social Action* on "Change Without War." Although he was strongly of the view that nuclear weapons were, for all intents and purposes, unusable and represented the threat of catastrophe for the human race, Herman Reissig was by no means a simplistic disarmer. Indeed, as will be seen from the essay below, he stated unequivocally:

> Armaments are not a cause of war. Nations do not fight because they have guns; they have guns because they are afraid or because they want what they cannot get without fighting. And simply to cry "Peace! Peace!" is really a waste of time.

(© *Social Action*, October, 1962)

Little did President Ronald Reagan know that when, in the 1980s, he expressed similar views in very similar words, Herman had said them already 20 years earlier.

But from the same point of departure, Reissig and Reagan diverged significantly. In Herman's opinion, the way forward lay in establishing workable, multilateral political and diplomatic machinery to deal with the challenges of international change. He developed his article on "Change Without War" into a chapter in his book *Man's New Home* published in 1964 by United Church Press. He concludes with these paragraphs:

I shall not hesitate to claim that those who take account of indubitable realities and work with patience and persistence to build structures for the maintenance of tolerable order and the settling of disputes are better servants of peace and goodwill than those who divide their time between protesting against armaments and calling for peace. Peace is a product of justice and of concrete political arrangements that prevent disputes from leading to war. It is not even certain that some of our prayers for peace and the hymns we sing in praise of it are helpful. For how can God give us peace in our time unless we work at the practical business of eliminating the causes of tension and building institutions for peaceful change? The much-maligned diplomat may sometimes be serving the goal of a better world more effectively than those who from some supposed higher "spiritual" level pour scorn on his endeavors.

Modern technology is making national control of armaments incompatible with human welfare. If this sounds shocking to some Americans we have only to think of some dictators of powerful nations in the contemporary world. How do we like the possibility that they might plunge the world into war? What about some ambitious Middle East government, hungry for imperial control and gradually acquiring the military capacity -- including nuclear weapons -- to carry out its designs? Do we like the prospect of the government of China in unrestrained control of nuclear armaments? Surely we would think it desirable if such national governments could somehow be deprived of the capability for war. But is it so certain that our own country can be trusted with armaments that can decide the fate of civilization? Even if the United States would never deliberately go to war except in self-defense, is it inconceivable that it might misjudge a situation, or that nationalistic fervor or anger might impair its judgment? What shall we say to the fact that in attempting to defend the national interest a nation using nuclear weapons takes into its hands, perhaps in fateful degree, the life of many other nations? This is the stark and terrible fact about nuclear war, that the national right to go to war really means the right to kill and destroy far beyond the boundaries of the offending nation. If the testing of nuclear weapons rightfully concerns nations whose opinions are not asked, how much more vitally would the use of such weapons concern them? Shall we leave the fate of the world to the decision of one nation? Or two?

It is, to be sure, one thing to say that the sovereign right of a nation to defend itself with arms assumes a radically new character when its arms are nuclear weapons that can destroy civilization. It is another, harder thing to say who or what should control the arms and make the decision about their use. But the way ahead will not be found unless we recognize that in the contemporary world -- with supersonic flight, man-made instrument-carrying planets whirling above the nations, and missiles carrying continental death -- it is blindness to talk about armaments in old nationalistic terms.

We must now work with all possible speed to establish the reign of international law, with a system of conciliation boards, equity tribunals, and courts, backed by an international police force. The achievement of such a system would be a giant step, and we must not underestimate the difficulties. But the real dreamers today are those who think the welfare of the new world can be served by the institutions of a world that is gone. Necessity has always been a mother of invention, and there is now laid upon us the clear necessity to invent institutions to take the place of war. The fact that scientific laboratories are more manageable than public opinion and parliaments only means that we must summon to our political tasks all the energy and resourcefulness of which we are capable. It does not mean that we have to sleepwalk into the defeat of civilization. Nor does the fact that a new system cannot be created in a few years mean that we should not be using far more brains, money, and energy for this task.

The great conflict between Communist nations and Western democracy is at a stage that makes the actual establishment of the needed institutions seem almost impossible in the next decades. But this conflict -- which will probably not be the last dangerous conflict between nations -- also provides a spur, since it writes upon the sky both the extreme danger of national armaments and the futility of efforts to abolish or even control them until there are new ways to protect the nations and to supervise change.

The tasks to which this chapter has pointed are immensely complicated. They require the hard, sustained thinking of experts in politics, economics, law, and other disciplines. The practical steps cannot be worked out in mass meetings, parades, sermons, or lectures in the churches. Making a landing on the moon and undertaking surgery on the human brain are, by comparison, almost simple. But the moral and religious forces of the nation have here a function and an obligation. They can wake up the almost sleeping conscience of the people on the moral and spiritual outrage of nuclear war. They can challenge, as they have not yet challenged, the mind that puts the nation above humanity and that, in Reinhold Niebuhr's phrase, makes the nation "the source of its ultimate moral norms." They can help to make clear to our people the basic facts of the new world situation. They can give strong support to those who in the universities, in government, and in professional organizations are working at the hard tasks of fashioning new policies for new situations.

(©*United Church Press*, 1964)

The Character and Uses of Power

In another Chapter from *Man's New Home*, Herman dealt with a subject troubling to Christians who have been taught to "turn the other cheek":

They need an orderly society; that is, a society in which the strong and the ruthless cannot with impunity hurt their neighbors and in which public services necessary to the person are reasonably well provided. Minorities in the society need protection against majorities, and majorities against ruthless minorities. The persons constituting a nation need protection against the destruction of their homes and institutions at the hands of other national groups. How do I, in love, meet such needs? Whatever may be the case in some other world, the answer for this world is clear enough. Moved by love, I will work for a social structure, including legal and police elements, without which these personal needs cannot be met. And if the policeman uses his club or his gun or the army moves into an area where order has broken down, shall we say that this has nothing of love in it? Is it not plain that to stand aside from force is sometimes to turn our backs on indubitable human needs? It cannot be true to say that as soon as coercion enters, love departs.

(©*United Church Press*, 1964)

(More complete excerpts from this chapter in *Man's New Home* can be found in Appendix II.)

The Meaning and Promise of the United Nations

With such a broad, international outlook on world affairs, it was not surprising that Herman Reissig regarded the concept of the United Nations with an approving eye. Moreover, for some years as secretary for international relations of the UCC's Council for Christian Social Action, he had an office on the ninth floor of the Church Center built on First Avenue at 44th street, immediately facing the United Nations. In very real terms, he had a ringside seat. While viewing the UN in a positive and constructive light, he was not blind to its defects and difficulties, nor was he totally uncritical. However, it was the organization's *potential*, rather than its current practice, that engaged him.

At that time, the UN was in its 19th year. From its original membership of 51 states, its membership was now 111.The great increase of new states emerging into independence from the era of colonialism and empire was in full swing. But it had already experienced major crises -- the war in Korea in the early 1950s, a large peacekeeping operation in the Congo in which the UN became embroiled in a fierce political disagreement between the USSR and the United States and their respective allies, the death in an air crash in 1961 of Secretary-General Dag Hammarskjold, the Cuban missile crisis of 1962, and the Arab-Israeli war of 1963. In such times, it was easy for the public to lose sight of the purpose and long-term objectives of the United Nations. Herman added his voice to those endeavoring to remind the public what the organization was all about. The excerpts that follow are taken from his article in the January 1, 1964 issue of the *United Church Herald*:

> About the UN's specific actions or failures to act there will always be differences of opinion. Criticism will never cease, as it should not. The most thoughtful friends of the organization do not urge us to "support the UN"; they advise what they like to call "discriminating support." And, like the Constitution of the United States, the UN Charter will no doubt be amended from time to time. Procedural rules will be changed. No one is wholly satisfied with the record or the present performance.
>
> The harsh attacks on the UN that are heard in many American communities stem from a source deeper than dismay over this or that UN policy or action. In the dedication ceremonies for the Church Center for the United Nations, U.S. Ambassador Adlai Stevenson said: "When we come to count our present-day blessings, I would put the United Nations, with all its shortcomings, high on the list."
>
> *An Idea Demanding Birth*
>
> The UN is not here because some visionaries or professional internationalists or world-planners liked the idea. It was not "sold" by a clever few to an inattentive multitude. It is not the child of Franklin D. Roosevelt or of any group of statesmen. The governmental leaders who met in San Francisco were midwives for an idea demanding birth. If anything in human affairs is inevitable, it seems inevitable that after the irrational and unlimited violence of the two wars the world's people would demand some new and creative attempt to abolish war. This was the genesis of the United Nations.

How could war be abolished? Surely, not by going on as before. Not by building nationally controlled armaments to be used when suasion has failed. National armed power might restrain this or that would-be aggressor at certain times and places, but the war system would remain. War can never be eliminated by preparing for war. This is a contradiction in terms and in fact.

It seems clear enough when one thinks hard about it that the world of nations will ultimately have to do what the people of a civilized nation do. They organize a system of laws, judicatories and police power for the settlement of disputes and the restraint of individual violence. The security of the individual in the domestic society is protected by the community. In the same way on the world level the whole community must organize itself for the restraint of international violence and for the protection of all the nations, great and small. If anarchy is defined as a state of society without government or law, we have to say that the world society exists in a state of near-anarchy.

The United Nations is a beginning. It does not work too well. The governments of the nations will not -- should not, cannot -- surrender their autonomy with respect to vital decisions until they can be reasonably sure of the ability of a larger political unit to protect their people and their interests. The nation is still, on the human level, the *prime* custodian of personal security. And there are unique values held by the national society for whose protection the national government is responsible. Hence the alarm felt by most of us when national sovereignty seems in any way threatened. "In God we trust." Yes, but also and of necessity our trust is in lesser powers such as the United States of America.

But there is a new situation. And this is what the opponents of the UN seem unable to grasp. The airplane started the process and the intercontinental ballistic missile, armed with an atomic warhead, finished it. *The nation can no longer protect its people.* Because of this fact, dimly or clearly recognized, fear has taken hold of our minds -- fear that sometimes approaches madness. The difference in our response to the UN lies precisely here. The awareness of our new and terrible insecurity leads some Americans to demand ever more and more military power. Their hope is in the weight and threat of incomparable armaments. By the same token, any international organization or commitment that seems to dilute our sovereignty (freedom of action) is met with vigorous resistance.

Another Perspective

The same awareness of the new situation leads other Americans to say something like this: Down the road of national military power and of unlimited national sovereignty there is no hope -- no hope at all, for Americans or for any other people. Even without actual war, the fantastic and ever-mounting cost of armaments and the subordination of increasing areas of the national life to military needs threaten to subvert the true ends of life. If we should ever resort to full-scale use of our weapons we would do far more than kill 20 or 50 or a 100 million people; we might do irreparable damage to the human spirit.

Our only hope, therefore, is in the slow but resolute building of international procedures and structures that look toward world order, justice and peace. National armaments and unlimited national sovereignty must begin to give way to international consultation and cooperation and to international instruments for settling controversies. In short, international anarchy must be replaced by an international order. And this will be accomplished, not exclusively but mainly through a permanent world organization that little by little grows in experience and in capacity to meet the needs that the nations can no longer by themselves supply.

In a short article much that needs to be said about the UN must be omitted. But there is one aspect of the meaning of the world organization that deserves more attention that it has received. The second paragraph of the Charter's opening words says that the peoples of the United Nations are determined "to reaffirm faith in fundamental human rights in the dignity and worth of the human person, in the equal rights of men and women of nations large and small."

I sometimes think that the way in which the human person is brought into the center may come to be the deepest value of the United Nations. To be sure, the UN is made up of nations, represented by their governments, not of individual persons. But the very fact that the organization is not national but international, almost worldwide, means that man as man is lifted up here. Walk through the corridors or into almost any meeting. Black, white, brown and every other color of the human race. Men and women from almost all the nations on earth. Rich nations, poor nations, big nations, tiny nations. East, West, North, South -- the human race, the family of man.

A nation is not universal; it is literally parochial, provincial. Political and economic systems are divided and divisive. No religious system is universal. Only God and the human person are truly universal. One visits the UN and has, more than in any other place on earth, a feeling of completeness. Here the national origin matters less, color not at all. Men and women of all the great religions are here. It feels *right*. Man, the human being, walks in the corridors and sits in the council chambers.

The nation-states have spelled out the rights of their people, from the English Magna Carta to the American Bill of Rights. It was the United Nations that, for the first time in history, gave the world a Universal Declaration of *Human* Rights. Day by day, year by year, insistently, this organization -- I almost called it a "movement" -- says, "Here is a man, a woman, a child. This is what is finally important. To the service of the human being, without regard to race, religion, economic status or political opinion, let us dedicate ourselves." For this reason, if for no other, the United Nations is in essence a powerful instrument of the Christian faith.

(©*United Church Herald*, January 1, 1964)

The Mature Christian in the Contemporary World

It is perhaps appropriate to conclude this chapter on "Politics and World Affairs" by quoting from Herman's book *Man's New Home* his definition of "The Mature Christian in a Contemporary World":

> He is a conservative, a liberal, and a progressive; and he tries not to be exclusively any one of these things.
>
> He is an individualist and a collectivist; and he does not think it makes sense in our kind of society to be consistently either one or the other.
>
> He is a patriot who loves the land where he was born and which has nourished him, and he is an internationalist who recognizes with Plato that above all nations is humanity; he recognizes also that in the contemporary world the nationalistic spirit cannot serve even the nation's people.
>
> He believes in personal responsibility and in social responsibility because he understands that society is nothing without persons, and persons are impossible without society.
>
> He believes in looking after himself and also in looking after his neighbor, especially the neighbor who needs someone to speak up for him.
>
> He believes we should do things for ourselves without help from government and also that we can use government in the interests of, and for the protection of, all of us.
>
> He believes in sharing his income through the church and other voluntary agencies and also through taxes.
>
> He believes in the widest possible area of freedom for individual thinking and action, and also in the necessity for laws and regulations that protect us from the unwise use of freedom.
>
> He believes that modern technology has made big industry, big labor, and big government unavoidable and that the threat of bigness to personal identity and freedom is too serious to waste time trying to meet it by going back to small industry, weak labor and little government.
>
> He is against communism and also against attempts to restore unregulated nineteenth-century capitalism.

He is in favor of preserving old ways and also in favor of change, depending on whether the welfare of persons seems to demand keeping old ways or inventing new ways.

He does not believe in giving unqualified support to any nation, political institution, or economic order, since all nations and social structures are highly imperfect instruments of service to God and man.

He believes in meeting contemporary problems with as few prejudgments as possible, trying only to be honest, intelligent, responsible, and loyal to the will of God as he understands it.

Photographer unknown

"If I cannot prevent the Communists from hating me, I can prevent the reactionaries from loving me."

Chapter IX. FREEDOM, VALUES AND SOCIAL JUSTICE

Edited by Derek Boothby,
Principal Officer, United Nations, and parishioner,
First Congregational Church of Greenwich,
Old Greenwich, Connecticut

As a lifelong liberal, Herman Reissig had a deep and unshakable belief in freedom. Freedom to think, to speak, to act, to live. At the same time he recognized that freedom often came at a high price and sometimes was out of reach for many of the world's human beings by reason of ideology, politics, economic hardship, the absence of social justice, bigotry, discrimination or other reasons of deprivation often beyond the control of the individual affected. By the same token, he was a spirited fighter in defense of the freedoms and values he held so dear.

From 1937 to 1942, he was the Executive Secretary of the Spanish Refugee Relief Campaign, headquartered in New York. They were difficult, challenging, exciting years. It was not surprising, given his liberal leanings, that he found himself in sympathy with the democratic Spanish Republican movement in its struggle for power against the Spanish fascists under the leadership of Generalissimo Franco. As the Spanish Civil War became ever more ugly and vicious, with Adolf Hitler giving military support to Franco, there were many liberals in North America and Western Europe who sought to find ways of assisting the Spanish Republican cause, either on the battlefields of Spain or by giving their support to refugees from the fighting.

A number of committees were established in the United States with the aim of coordinating efforts to raise funds, provide food and shelter, arrange medical assistance and so on. Attracting support from many quarters, all shades of the politically centrist and left spectrum became involved -- including Communists. By 1940, Herman Reissig found himself deeply involved in internecine political struggles for the control of the efforts in northeastern USA to provide assistance to the refugees and their movement in Spain which, by this time, was losing in the war.

Extracts from some of his letters of the period illuminate Reissig's position:

> . . . I and some members of our Board were on the point of withdrawing from the Spanish Refugee Relief Campaign because of the determined efforts of politically-minded people to control it. . . . Generally, I don't think we ought to leave potentially good, useful organizations to the Communists. We ought to take the organizations away from *them* -- and tell the world what we have done.
>
> (March 9, 1940)

> My somewhat intensive experience with the Communists, however, leads me to two conclusions: First, the Communists, in my opinion, do not initiate or associate themselves with an organization without a serious attempt to keep its control altogether in their own hands. Second, the Communists are primarily politicians and propagandists, and therefore their primary interest in any ostensibly humanitarian organization is its possible use on behalf of their cause. . .
>
> (October 2, 1940)

> You seem to think that because some of us once worked with the Communists we should work with them now, and because they did good work in a united front on behalf of Spain they deserve the support and confidence of all real liberals ad infinitum. . . .These are horribly difficult days for an anti-fascist. I am doing my darndest to steer a straight line. The Communists make it harder because any line that is not 100% their line is a crooked line. But, if I cannot prevent the Communists from hating me, I can prevent the reactionaries from loving me.
>
> (January 16, 1941)

Communism

That the reactionaries were, indeed, far from loving Herman Reissig soon became all too apparent. The Special House Committee on Un-American Activities, otherwise known as the Dies Committee after its chairman Representative Martin Dies, had been formed in 1938 to carry out an investigation of the extent, character and objects of subversive and un-American propaganda activities in the United States. Borne along on the crest of crusading zeal, the Dies Committee set out to expose communist and fascist influences in the United States. By 1942, its waves of accusatory condemnation were crashing down on many liberal organizations and individuals classified by Dies as communist fronts. Many liberals found themselves arbitrarily guilty by association.

On June 25, 1942, a special report was submitted to the House of Representatives entitled *Subversive Activities Aimed at Destroying Our Representative Form of Government*, (Union Calendar No. 812, Report 2277). Directed primarily at the Union for Democratic Action, the report contained details and a chart purporting to show the affiliations of the leaders of the UDA with the agencies and fronts of the Communist Party. Herman Reissig was listed as being associated with eleven of them. In his papers there is a copy of the Dies Report with markings in the margin in his own handwriting; eight times he wrote "no" where his name appeared, and at the foot of the page the notation: "8 of 11 wrong."

Six months earlier, in January 1942, Reissig had become the pastor of the First Union Congregational Church in Quincy, Illinois. On the Sunday following the release of the Dies Report, he led a short service of worship then announced that he would give the benediction, dismiss the regular service and have a statement to make to his congregation. Speaking from the floor of the church, Rev. Reissig made a detailed statement of more than a hour covering every phase of the circumstances that led to his being named in the report.

According to the report published in the *Quincy Herald-Whig* of June 29, 1942, after the statement there was spontaneous and prolonged cheering. A vote of confidence was passed unanimously, as were the following resolutions:

"Resolved, that the members of the First Union Congregational Church of Quincy, Illinois, deeply regret that statements made by the Dies Committee and published in the *Chicago Daily Tribune* concerning our minister have disturbed some of the people of Quincy, and we further deplore the necessity thus apparently forced upon Mr. Reissig of making a reply, and

"Be it further resolved that none of his acts or deeds warrant anything but the highest praise as a leader, and a good American citizen, and we approve of all he has done, and

"Be it further resolved that this congregation go on record with a vote of complete confidence in his Christian ministry and patriotic citizenship."

The vigor with which his congregation rejected the charges against him must have been very satisfying to Herman, standing alone before his judges on that Sunday morning. There can also be no doubt that the entire experience reaffirmed his beliefs in the freedoms and values by which he placed such great store.

Eighteen years later, on 23 June 1960, Reissig published an article, "This Is Also Subversive", in the *United Church Herald* which is reproduced here in part:

> Let us consider one particular threat to freedom in the United States. The threat - and it is a serious one - lies in the attempt to impose on all of us uniformity of belief in respect to political, economic, racial and other social problems. Sometimes the attempt even includes theological beliefs. This attempt sometimes takes the form of pinning the label "subversive" or "pro-Communist" on all who take positions with which some persons and some organizations do not agree.
>
> Against this attempt the churches ought to make the most vigorous kind of protest. Ministers and social action leaders ought to educate the people in our churches on the nature and meaning of this attempt. For this is, as I have said, a serious matter. We are dealing with a triple threat -- a threat to

freedom, a threat to American ideals and a threat to important Christian values. . . . . .

Early in the year 1936 the Russian Government promulgated a new Constitution that seemed to promise a greater freedom under communism. The terrible "purges," in which Stalin killed thousands of his political opponents after sham confessions and sham trials, did not occur until the late Thirties.

The early part of that decade was the time of the Great Depression in the United States. Millions were unemployed. Even generally conservative people were raising serious questions about the "capitalistic" economic system. The right of labor to organize was not yet accepted.

It was also the period when fascism and nazism were a great and growing threat to freedom and to peace. Germany, Austria and Italy were under the control of brutal and war-like Fascist governments. Fascist movements were numerous and prominent in the United States, as well as in England and France. In the summer of 1936 Fascists, led by Generalissimo Francisco Franco, with the support of Hitler and Mussolini, started a war against the Republican-democratic government of Spain.

This, then, was the situation at the time the organizations we are discussing were started. It was a time of widespread suffering and discontent, a time of alarm about the domestic and international threat of fascism, a time when communism, much as most Americans rejected it, was not by any means the powerful and obvious threat that it later became. . . . . .

These organizations had all kinds of purposes. They were created to fight war and fascism, to defend civil liberties, to give aid to the foreign born, to explore the grounds of friendship with the Soviet Union, to help save the Spanish Republic, to provide new homes for refugees from Fascist countries. Some of them were very small; some had tens of thousands of supporters. Some were short-lived; others are still in existence.

What is the authority for saying that some of these organizations were, or are, "subversive"? About a year after the end of World War II it became apparent that the hoped-for peaceful cooperation between the Soviet Union and its wartime allies would not be continued. A new kind of war then began -- the Cold War between the Soviet Union and the Western democracies. The United States was forced, slowly and reluctantly, to see that it had a new and dangerous struggle on its hands. The attention of our country was now turned to the new threat and its domestic, as well as foreign, representatives. . . . . .

The Government, therefore, instituted various "loyalty programs" and "loyalty tests." The Truman loyalty program of 1947 included a provision requiring the Attorney General to draw up a list of organizations that, on examination, he considered to have "subversive purposes." . . . . .

Were, or are, the organizations in fact subversive? The answer to this question requires a highly discriminating judgment. It is necessary to such judgment to say, at the outset, that all of these organizations had perfectly legitimate and perfectly good American purposes, so far as the average person could tell. One must go a step farther and say that these organizations did in actual fact do much work that was not only unobjectionable but highly laudable. They exposed and fought fascism and nazism. It would have been well if more Americans had awakened earlier to the menace of those movements.

They exposed and fought racial bigotry. They befriended the foreign-born -- of all political persuasions. They came to the defense of the Spanish Republic. Would that more Americans had done so! Many decent, loyal, intelligent Americans gave money to these organizations, attended meetings, gave permission for the use of their names. . . . . .

Why do some people so casually and in such wholesale fashion use the labels "Communist," "Communistic," "subversive"? The reason is clear. If their sole objective were to stop attempts to change our form of government by unconstitutional means and to substitute a Communist social order, they would be careful to center their attack on those who actually are trying to do this. By the wholesale and irrational character of their charges they prove that their objective is not merely to eliminate Communists but to discredit persons and organizations they do not like.

Lacking any really sound arguments, and in their blind fury, they look around for the ugliest charge they can find. The ugliest word in contemporary American society is the word "Communist." The fact that persons and organizations on whom the label is pinned have nothing whatever in common with communism seems irrelevant. One wants to eliminate their influence. The simplest way to do it is to cry: "Communistic! Subversive!"

To our shame, it must be said that many of us are such poor exponents of honest, fair-dealing, courageous, independent Americanism that as soon as anyone cries "Communist!" we shrink and cower and decide to play safe.

What a humiliating shame it is that the National Council of Churches should feel compelled to assure the American public that it has always been opposed to communism! What kind of people have we become, that such a dedicated Christian as Edwin T. Dahlberg should be denied the use of a Christian church because some ignorant and bitter persons wave before the church officers a list of allegedly subversive organizations to which he is alleged to have belonged!

One aspect of this matter, it may be remarked in passing, is strange indeed. Or perhaps not so strange as revealing! It is often the very people who are usually most suspicious of government who, when an agency of government gives them material for an attack on other Americans, leap to embrace the material and spread it around as gospel truth!

One final comment. A good reason for repudiating Communist philosophy and practice is the fact that Communists were originally responsible for poisoning the American atmosphere with the habit of suspicion and misrepresentation. Communists were and are "subversive" in that they propose to change our political system through underhand and unconstitutional means. Communists have lied about their membership in the Communist party.

They have tried to undermine democracy behind a front of concern for democracy. They have given the rest of us some kind of excuse for suspicion, hysteria and timidity.

But if Communists misrepresent and falsify, all the more reason why we should not do these things! It comes to this: one of the most effective ways in which an American can help to dissolve the most valuable American principles and can help the Communist cause is to cry "Communist" against persons and organizations he does not like, or to keep silent when good Americans and Christian leaders are maligned.

It is time Americans, and particularly American Christians, resisted the effort to make us conform. It is time we stopped running. It is time we recovered our souls.

(©*United Church Herald*, June 23, 1960)

Discrimination

There seem to have been several occasions in Herman's life, arising from some event or some thought that occurred to him, when he subjected himself to the rigors of his own intellectual introspection -- and found himself wanting.

Here is an essay, "I Have Sworn Eternal Hostility to Every Form of Discrimination," published in the *United Church Herald* on February 7, 1963, which is of particular interest when placed side by side with another essay that follows:

> I have just finished reading an important book. Leon Uris, in the novel *Mila 18*, tells the story of the extermination of the Jews by the Nazis in 1943. The author declares: "Within a framework of basic truth, tempered with a reasonable amount of artistic license, the places and events described actually happened." This is apparent to the reader.
>
> A week earlier I had read *Fight for Freedom* by Langston Hughes. This book tells some of the story of what white Americans have done to Negroes and of the struggle of the Negroes for recognition of their rights as human beings and as American citizens.
>
> I had not really wanted to read either of the books, thinking that I was already sufficiently impressed – and

depressed – by the agony of the Jewish and Negro peoples. The acclaim given *Mila* 18 and the literary distinction of Langston Hughes overcame my reluctance.

The reading of the books was a shaking experience. For the interpretation of human wickedness and human suffering -- on such a scale -- I have no adequate theology. One thought recurred again and again: it is, so it seemed to me, a wonder that so many Jews, even among the surviving witnesses of the Nazi extermination effort, still turn to God in prayer and that so many Negroes still have faith in the possibility of justice at the hands of God and of the white man.

Those of us whose roots run deep into the Christian faith and the Christian experience may say that the persistence of faith in a wise and loving God, despite bottomless depths of woe inflicted by man upon man, proves that God is and that he will not let us go. Or, we may cling to faith because it seems better to believe -- and so help to give the human story a chance to issue in glory -- than to yield to despair and, by yielding, make human defeat certain.

But if some sensitive men and women have seen and felt more woe than could in their minds be reconciled with faith in a divine providence and have decided to "curse God and die" or, as is the case of a larger number, have decided to live as best they can without religious faith, the rest of us can at least understand and refrain from judgment. The New Testament seems to support the conclusion that it is better to be agnostic and work for mercy and justice than to say "I believe" and take no part in the struggle against injustice.

This brings us to the main point of what I, moved by the two books, have wanted to say. Thomas Jefferson made a vow that has become a part of our national heritage: "I have sworn upon the altar of God eternal hostility to every form of tyranny over the mind of man."

If this seems a noble and stirring utterance, it may not be inappropriate for a contemporary American to speak with Jeffersonian accent and say: "I have sworn upon the altar of God eternal hostility to every form of discrimination against human beings on grounds of race or religion." Some such vow, I submit, every responsible person, and especially every Christian, ought now to make.

Reviewing the history of the Western world, the English writer, H.G.Wells, said: "Race prejudice is the worst, the very worst thing in the world." It is a statement of fact. Race prejudice is evil, in that it has no good or acceptable aspects. It is full-charged sin against God and man. The moral indictment of race prejudice has no loopholes.

War is an evil thing. But some wars have had some good results. Men's objectives in going to war have sometimes been good objectives, even if the means used wrought incalculable moral and physical harm. Race prejudice has produced no good. Its motivations cannot stand the light of reason or good will.

Communism, in some of its manifestations, does great injury to human life. But the motives of many Communists are noble motives. Communist societies can be credited with some worthwhile achievements. Race prejudice never helped anyone. The motives that impel men to kill Jews and Negroes or to bar them from full exercise of their human rights are not acceptable motives.

Liquor has ruined untold numbers of men and women. But the evil is not in the liquor; it is in its misuse by individuals and in the corrupting influence of the commerce in liquor. Race prejudice is in essence an expression of human sin. On both the prejudiced and their victims it works pure injury.

Gambling does much harm to individuals and to society. But some gambling is harmless and the urge to gamble has in it some innocent or even useful human traits. Race prejudice is never harmless; its mildest expressions help to poison human relations. The really shocking expressions of anti-semitism or of white supremacy would not be possible without the widespread existence of "mild" prejudice.

Obscenity in speech and writing is deplorable. But the book that incites lust in one person may in another arouse only mild interest, disdain or disgust. All the "dirty" writing ever published has done no harm to be compared with the results of bias.

Human sin expresses itself in varied ways. Evil takes on many forms. The man in whose heart there is awe before God and respect for his fellow man will fight on many fronts. But there is one battle whose lines are clear, one battle to which all men of good will should commit themselves utterly and without compromise -- the battle against racial prejudice.

The wounds inflicted by antisemitism and by the doctrine of white superiority are spiritually so awful in the number of lives destroyed that no human atonement is possible. Contemplating what these evils have accomplished, the only response must be an inner trembling and a personal vow of "eternal hostility to every form of discrimination against human beings on grounds of race or religion."

(©*United Church Herald*, February 7, 1963)

The other essay, "I am a Racist," was written about two years later:

I am a United Church of Christ minister, white, liberal and retired. Black militants call me a racist. I look back on my record in race relations to discover how this could be. ......

Until a few months ago I rejected the charge. The allegation made me feel sad. So I dismissed white racism as an understandable but still grossly exaggerated and unfair accusation, the kind of name-calling to which the angry are prone.

Since whites as a whole had treated blacks very badly for 300 years, I was not going to be put off if justified black anger included unfairness toward me and others who had worked as hard and as wisely as we could to rid our society of the curse of racial discrimination and injustice.

I kept cool and went on working. I refused to criticize even the most belligerent black leaders. The white liberal's business, I felt and publicly said, was not to find fault with blacks but to try to change the attitudes and practices of whites.

But last spring I began to wake up. Many books and articles *by* black militants helped me to understand. Reading *about* them in the newspapers was one thing; their carefully written publications presented a different picture. . . . . . .

Like so many others, I had worked for "racial integration." But what would this integration have meant in practice?

I now admit that it meant Negroes would be integrated into the dominant culture. This culture had been fashioned by white people -- churches, educational institutions, politics, moral standards, entertainment industries, recreational facilities.

Integration was a one-way street. It meant black people coming to us white people, fitting in, adjusting themselves to something they had practically no part in creating. . . . . .

I now recognize that we have expected Negroes to play an essentially passive role -- which is indicated by our favorite words "accept" and "accepted." Other white people and I would *accept* black men and women. This was my unconscious and unexamined assumption.

Consider how this assumption was expressed in organized religion. How often, in speaking to church groups about race relations, has some earnest church member voiced his puzzlement: "In our church we have made it clear that we would be glad to have Negroes attend the services and join the church if they want to. But they don't come. Do they, after all, prefer to be by themselves?"

I am now appalled when I recall my response. I only suggested additional steps white churches could take to persuade Negroes to "come." If ever I advised white people to "go" it was only to go as occasional visitors demonstrating white friendliness. . . . . .

It would not occur to most white Christians to attend a Negro church regularly, much less to join it. Why then should we expect Negroes to feel at home in white churches? If integration became a two-way street, both races might profit and each could feel at home in the other's churches.

The white liberal's flagrant assumptions in church life have been operative also in all parts of our culture. We thought it enough that black boys and girls should be accepted in white-run educational institutions. We were surprised, dismayed and shocked when black students and professors asked for some changes in curriculum and administration! Most of us white people never dreamed that *we would need to make some adjustments.*

There is no getting around it: *I have been a racist.* Not in the overtly ugly way of some white people, Northern and Southern, but in the subtle, hard-to-change sense of proposing to be an accepter of black people and never asking if I and my white ways could -- or should -- be accepted by blacks.

Mine is the deep-rooted psychological and spiritual racism of the liberal white American. I am therefore thankful for the shock treatment given to me by black militants. Intellectually acute victims, they have seen what I could not see -- and still do not see very clearly.

As I now begin to understand, my racism cannot be quickly and cleanly exorcised. For I live and move and have my being in a social structure created and maintained by whites. This structure is not simply Western; it is white. Neither African nor American blacks have been on the inside helping to create it.

Except as they became Uncle Toms, American blacks could get nowhere near the sources of power. In order to get ahead or just to survive, some black Americans have surrendered their unique characteristics, their dignity and worth as black people. They have striven to be as much as possible like white people, even to the point of hating their color.

As articulate blacks are now telling the white world, the exquisite crime of the whites is that they made the American Negro hate himself. In this crime the white liberal has participated by his unconscious racism.

At this point I anticipate an objection from my liberal Christian friends. They will say that whiteness and blackness are not really important. We are all human beings and children of God. We must forget our skin color and accept each other simply as human beings.

In more than one speech and article I have myself maintained that a Christian must be color blind. Alas, for my unconscious racism!

Being a member of the white dominant race and of its social structure, I took my conception of a human being from that of ambience. The visual image (one must have some visual image in order to think about human beings) was *white*. If ever I had thought about it, I would not have imagined color-blind black Christians seeing me *black*.

No, it won't do to be color blind. This is asking both whites and blacks to forget and suppress a part of their human heritage.

Such a request is like suggesting that a woman cease being a woman and a man stop being a man because both are human beings. As a woman must accept herself as a woman if she is to have a satisfactory relationship with the male population, so black people must accept themselves as black people, rejoice in their blackness, and see black as beautiful. *Only in this way can there eventually be an acceptable integration of the races.*

The other side of this truth is the inability of whites to put themselves in the black person's shoes. When we white men understand our racism as "given," when black men fully accept their race, and when both respect each other's uniqueness and worth, then the two races may be able to live together without fear or hostility.

But we are a long way from that day.

(Essay, December, 1964)

As he grew older, Herman continued to challenge himself and those around him. Ever the Christian curmudgeon, he asked the awkward questions, made the probing comments and tackled the difficult issues. In one form or another, the themes of freedom, values and social justice often appeared in his sermons and writings.

Humanism

In the early 1970s, he wrote about Humanism in his column, "Something to Think About" where he pointed out that Christians should not only be savers of souls, but savers of lives:

> This is the first main meaning of humanism: the essentially human is always interesting and important, whatever the name, nation, race, religion, or personal character. So the humanist reads the Bible, but also Dickens, Faulkner, Hemingway, Henry Miller, George Bernard Shaw. He reads religious periodicals, but also secular magazines and the newspapers. He wants to know about the churches, even if he never enters one, because they represent an important aspect of the human scene. But he also pays attention to politics, education, art, science. If anything is human, he wants to at least have some understanding of it, even if it does not personally appeal to him. We say of some people that they are "highly cultured," by which we mean that they know something about every prominent aspect of human life, past and present. We could as well say that such people are "real humanists."
>
> A second essential character of humanism is in its respect for the worth and dignity of the human person. The humanist cares more for people than for theories, money, institutions. He supports what contributes to human happiness and growth and opposes what hurts men, women and children. He hates war, racial discrimination, economic exploitation because of the suffering they inflict on people. He abhors slums, not because slums do not look nice (though they are ugly) but because a child brought up in a slum has two strikes against him before he knows what is happening to him. He is horrified by our prisons, not because he views crime lightly, but because a person who has committed a crime remains a human being and has therefore basic rights that must be respected.
>
> The humanist is an internationalist, not because he does not love his own country, but because all people are members of one human family, deserving our respect and our concern.

If the death of an American soldier is tragic, so is the death of any soldier of any nation. The wife, or mother, of a dead North Vietnamese soldier will cry as hard as the mother or wife of an American soldier. The color or nationality or politics of the corpse is not, for the humanist, a sufficient reason for deciding whether to care or not to care.

Perhaps the most important thing going on in the churches today is the rediscovery of the humanism of the Christian religion. The churches are learning to pay attention to education, politics, art, science, housing, income levels, economic practices. That is to say, they begin to understand their responsibility for man's common, everyday life.

Our churches will not be truly Christian churches until they work for man's welfare in this world as well as in the next, until, in short, they become Christian humanists.

(©*The Ledger*, date unknown)

Social Justice

As Pastor Emeritus of First Congregational Church, Old Greenwich, Connecticut, some of his words did not always sit easily upon the ears of some of his congregation in that materially well-upholstered community. Such discomfort was, of course, precisely what Herman was aiming at as he sought to exclude no one, certainly not himself, from his thought- provoking strictures.

On December 9, 1984, Herman presented what was to be his last sermon. The topic was "Social Justice as a Road to Peace" and, well into his eighty-sixth year, his thunder was as loud as ever. Here are some extracts:

> In pondering the basis and meaning of justice it became clear to me that the concept of justice has no meaning apart from the conviction that all human beings, just by being human, have an inherent and immeasurable worth. The American Declaration of Independence expresses this in saying, "We hold these truths to be self-evident: that all men are created equal and that they are endowed by their creator with certain unalienable rights." The Bible says it by

asserting that all human beings are the children of God. You can't take human heritage higher than that.

Is it possible really to believe that? All the millions and billions who have lived in misery and died in obscurity, all the millions who have been slaughtered in war, all the fly-pestered beggars of Bombay, all the Ethiopians who as we meet here today are dying of hunger, all the drug addicts and the drug pushers -- all of these have an immeasurable worth, all are ennobled by being the offspring of God? How can anyone believe that? No, dear St. Paul, when you wrote, "Now are we all the children of God," you had a beautiful theory that won't stand up under realistic scrutiny.

And yet, this belief in human worth is the foundation of all morality; if you let go of it, justice is a lovely superstructure without foundation. And what gives the worth that must be respected? Certainly not your nice clothes, your fine house, your real estate or money in the bank. These are as grass, which today is green and tomorrow withers. If I have worth superior to a rabbit it is because, as a human being, I have something you can call mind, or spirit, or soul. And all human beings have that, however underdeveloped they may be. All human beings are therefore bound together in one great solidarity; we stand or fall together. So it's true: all men are created equal.

Now we can see what justice is. To deal justly means, first, that you fully recognize the high worth of your human neighbor and, second, that you make such practical arrangements as will help the neighbor to develop his or her highest potential. When you, knowingly or unknowingly, use a human neighbor primarily for your benefit without regard to the neighbor's well-being you are acting unjustly. When a national society or a world society elevates some people while holding other people down, that is social injustice.

. . . . . The prevailing social structure can make good people do bad things. I am sometimes pulled up sharp by the thought that I, with my mainly good intentions, may be practicing injustice, or at least assenting to injustice because it is a part of the society in which I live. For example, I once told stories and sang songs that clearly denigrated black people. To adapt words spoken to his congregation by that superlative Christian preacher William Sloane Coffin, I did not get up in the morning asking, "Whom can I insult and exploit today?" I did, nevertheless, insult and exploit black people because I was enmeshed in a culture that had not yet waked up to the gross injustice of using black people for the benefit of white people.

I offer now three theses leading to this conclusion:

1. The seeds of all violent revolutions are sown by those at the top of society who practice injustice toward those at the bottom.
2. When those at the bottom of society begin to recognize that they too are fully human and therefore have human rights, they always begin demanding redress of their grievances by peaceful means: petitions, marches, peaceful assemblies.
3. When, after years of pleading and petitioning, the oppression, instead of lifting, becomes more severe, the patience of the oppressed runs out and they reach for clubs and guns.

Therefore: If today we wish to avoid both bloody revolutions and totalitarian communism we should keep alert to situations of injustice wherever they occur, and do what we can, individually, through corporate action and through our government, to help liberate the oppressed from the injustice practiced against them. Justice should be our first concern. . . . . .

Consider Central America -- Guatemala, Nicaragua, El Salvador. The history and the present situation are complicated and one must not oversimplify. The root of the matter runs like this: in all of those countries illiteracy and poverty runs very high. A small group in each country is wealthy and has built glittering cities. Around every splendid city in Central America, as also in South America, are the barrios where live hundreds of thousands who pick in garbage cans for food and live in shanties. Most of the wealth is produced by export of coffee, sugar, cotton, bananas. Most of the profit goes to the elite in those countries and to the United States. The common people in Central America get very little of it. There lies the root of revolution in Latin America. All the world knows that Americans are anti-communist. Much of the world is not sure the United States stands for social justice.

From several sources we learn that between thirty-five and forty million Americans live in families below the poverty line. Someone says that the poorest in the United States are usually better off than most of the people in Africa or even in the Soviet Union. That may be so, but we're talking about our fabulously rich country.

What is to be done? What are the practical political and economic steps we can take to see that there is a more just distribution of wealth? We have the brains, the ingenuity, the technology. What most Americans apparently still lack is simple moral revulsion against almost sybaritic luxury at the top of society while at the bottom millions scratch for a bare existence. The Catholic bishops are right; the present unequal distribution of wealth is "morally unacceptable."

You are not sure you agree? Well, once most did not agree that infanticide was evil. Once most did not think burning heretics was wrong. Once most people accepted the system of slavery. Once child labor in factory and mine was acceptable.

Today the spirit of God is asking us to say "NO!" to our greatest social evils: the piling up of nuclear arms, and poverty in the midst of plenty.

O, my well-fed, well-clothed, well-housed self, and you, my dear well-fed, well-clothed, well-housed neighbors, let us listen to God's prophets and to the Prince of Peace: Justice and only justice shall you seek.

(Sermon, December 9, 1984)

Photographer unknown

Herman Reissig was on divine assignment to keep attuned to what is happening in the world with antennae perked to God's work of justice and peace.

Chapter X. IN MEMORIAM

Reflections on the Life of the Rev. Dr. Herman F. Reissig
by the Rev. R. Alan Johnson , Sunday, June 23, 1985
First Congregational Church of Greenwich

How Herman would have loved to be here in person, to preach, and not to avoid adulation, humbly. Also, he'd have liked to hear the music which substitutes wings for plodding feet and wipes the dust from our spirits. I will use many of Herman's words in this celebration of his life.

One of God's prophetic correspondents has died. You see, Herman was on divine assignment to keep attuned to what is happening in the world with antennae perked to God's work of justice and peace. Then Herman gave us interim reports through sermons, and voluminous letters, in discussion at meals and even Second Hours; through judiciously crafted words at baptisms and funerals and weddings; at ordinations and parties, he got to us, prophetically reporting on God's work in the world and our part in it. He touched head and heart -- moving us to tears and chuckles and belly laughs; to disagreement and disturbance and assent; to challenge and change. He got inside us with his prophetic voice.

Abraham Heschel writes "a prophet is one who interferes." So Herman told us: Justice and only justice shall you seek. In speaking truth in love, let us remember that love may require speaking unpalatable truths. So the present administration in Washington (and how could we not refer to this on Herman's behalf) stands judged as dangerous. A prophet looks at the present with critical eyes and a gospel vision. So it was Herman's assignment to be one of God's prophetic correspondents. Damn the secular world's torpedoes -- full speed ahead! He charged.

Herman stirred us and he got underneath the surface, not to *hurt* but to expose what is true. He summed up his advice this way: "be young all your life and say things to the world that are true."

And just within this year he wrote, "my ears are age 98, my eyes are age 75, but I can keep my spirit at age 30." He was not a natural believer, but, in his words, one who cries from the depths rather than sings from a mountain top. The Biblical character Jacob wrestled at the Jabbok with the Angel, wresting meaning. Herman was such a *God-wrestler*; one who had the fire of mind and emotion to stir and feed us in our depths.

If we do not find ourselves struggling more with how our faith makes sense in this radically changed world; or how our religious language can more adequately convey new truths; or how accommodation with the status quo is in itself a death; or how to be constructively at odds with society, then we've still not heard this prodding, sometimes irascible prophetic voice.

Thanks be for the Catholic Bishops' letters on peace and economic justice and for the words of Schillebeeckx, particularly. These fed Herman's thinking heart of late and underscored again his uneasy love of the church. He wrote, "all Christians ought to agree . . . moral responsibility entails political responsibility and therefore a church that stands aloof from politics is not responsibly carrying out its mission." Herman led us not to avoid prickly subjects. This he did to ennoble, not denigrate; to use his mind in the service of Christ. Out of *friendship* he interfered. He wrote, "there is salt and vinegar as well as sugar in friendship." True friendship includes candor. He lauded friends who do not limit their response to compliments, although he did decide against the following as a possible book title: *Letters to Conservatives and Other Sinners*. Herman could be prophetic with all ages and persons with very differing beliefs because he was also a lover of persons.

Herman exhibited vigilant attention to language: "Do not muffle your words"; a summons to an athletic intellect: "Don't skimp on hard thinking"; an invitation to voracious reading: "Let us sit at the feet of scholars"; and showed a penetrating wit to undo whatever was false: "What's the point of driving in the fast lane if the road goes to no good place?"

Herman's theology is theocentric humanism. "I became a watcher and student of human life", he wrote, that is to say, a pastor/preacher, an asker of questions about who we are and why we are as we are and what the future may hold for us. For faith to be alive it had to be explicated in warm, human terms. No theological pablum endured. So when words today tend to laminate our souls with verbal plastic, Herman's word was to wake us so as to be captivated and fascinated by being human.

"Human life," he wrote,"is an awesome thing and my passion is to find new and better ways to keep the sense of its greatness, immortality or no immortality, God or no God." He exhorted us to"keep earthy with Jesus." Herman was known for his repugnance of mediocre theology which sentimentalizes God and flaccid words which make Jesus bloodless. He confessed that "Lincoln, Gandhi and Einstein are all a part of my inner being because they convey the powerful spirit of Jesus, the one who was fully human."Herman, divine wrestler with those who have clay feet, living his convictions that the demand for a transcendent meaning does not die. It cannot die because it is the essence of what it means to be human. God is at the center of the search to be human.

Once when Herman came to preach at the church I served in Sharon, Ct, he asked to borrow a white shirt. After the service, my wife asked if Herman realized the shirt was the one I wore when she and I were married. Herman retorted, "well, yes, this morning I did feel *particulary warm*." A man of passion, he was connected to the *earth* through his tomatoes, and strawberries; to *eros* through books and daffodils, hyacinths and tulips; to *agape* through his family as in his admission, "grand-parentage is my favorite occupation," and to the *Holy Spirit* through friends, conversation, music, poetry, *Christianity and Crisis*, and *The New York Times*.

He declared: Get up and go on. Death is real but life is stronger. Quoting Unammuno he troubled us with this benediction: "May God deny you peace and grant you glory." Glory time has come for Herman as well as peace at the last.

The final words Herman spoke to me at the hospital two weeks ago tonight as I paced around nervously; leaned over to speak and to hear; held his hand, were: "Relax, Alan, I'll be fine in the morning." The Psalmist's words shine through these words: "Weeping tarries for the night, but joy comes in the morning."

I miss Herman terribly. And still we rejoice; we thank God for Herman. One of God's prophetic correspondents has finished this part of his assignment.

Martha B. Porter, photographer

"Yours for creating moral excitement in a dark Nixonian world."

BLESSINGS AND BENEDICTIONS

These are the ways of "signing off" which Herman Reissig used in his letters (1974-1978)

A warm salute,

Yours for creating moral excitement in a dark Nixonian world,

Agape plus,

Keep the banners flying, love,

Yours until we can "splash at a ten-league canvas with brushes of comet's hair,"

Yours for more joie de vivre,

Yours ad infinitum but I hope not ad nauseam,

Yours, praying for courage,

Allons,

The sun is bright today -- may there be brightness in your soul,

Yours for keeping a stiff upper lip when it is impossible to smile,

Sing praises and clasp hands,

May the Lord defend you in body and protect you spiritually,

May you have the grit and grace you need,

Yours always hoping,

Yours believing that "tasks in hours of insight willed can be in hours of gloom fulfilled,""

Strugglingly and hopefully yours,

Yours toward the rising sun,

Yours "in the boundary" between despair and hope -- but always with more hope than despair,

So, I will end this outpouring by saying to myself and to you: Come on! Let's get going. And with God be the rest,

God be thanked for hours of pain and also for hours of happiness and delight,

Yours, enduring today's sluggish hours and expecting brighter hours tomorrow -- or later today,

Yours frustrated by the armament race -- and damning it,

Yours, needing to live much longer in order to acquire a little wisdom,

Yours in all kinds of weather,

Yours always getting up and going on,

Turning now to the work of paying monthly bills, I am your obedient and willing servant,

Yours crying out of the depths and seeing some stars,

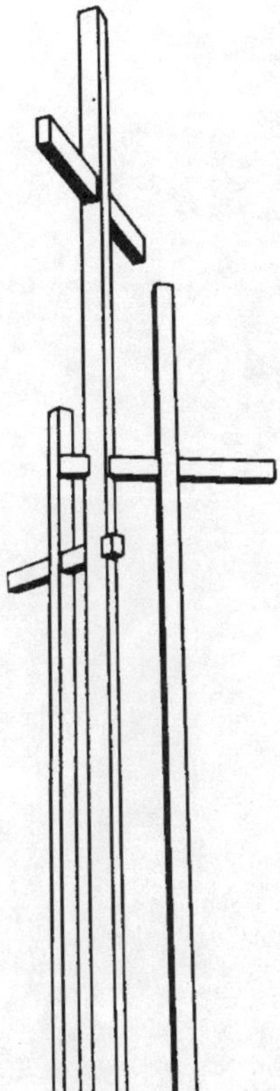

Martha B. Porter, Photographer

"My God wants us to align ourselves with a moving toward justice and mutual aid. My God is a great magnet that keeps drawing me back toward his purposes."

APPENDIX I

INTRODUCTION TO THREE SELECTED SERMONS

Characteristics of a Good Church III, October 10, 1982

What Does It Mean to Believe in God?, October 9, 1983

Singing the Lord's Song in a Foreign Land, May 6, 1984

Herman Reissig was as vital and current in his last years as he was in his earlier life—perhaps even more so. The three sermons included here in their entirety were all written and delivered in the last few years of his life. They have been chosen to illustrate the strength and clarity of his thoughts and beliefs that had been formulated over six decades.

As those of you who knew him read these sermons, we hope that you will visualize his presence, hear his voice delivering the words and remember how, through his own powerful oratorical style and conviction, he gripped us, helped us see things more clearly and often made us squirm.

Herman spoke from the depths of his heart and mind without "pulling any punches." Yet, because of his sincerity, he was perhaps loved and respected more by those who disagreed with some of his liberal positions than by those who agreed with them.

One of his last sermons, "Singing the Lord's Song in a Foreign Land," received the 1987 Connecticut Conference (UCC) Peace Center Preaching Award. Herman concluded this sermon with these words:

> We can say *no* to the hawks and join the doves, and not be intimidated when we are called unrealistic, naive, or unpatriotic. In such ways, and in many other ways, we can sing the Lord's song in a foreign land.

CHARACTERISTICS OF A GOOD CHURCH III

Sermon by Rev. Dr. Herman F. Reissig

October 10, 1982

Let us now think together about one more characteristic of a good church. *A good church is a church that is conspicuous for goodness and compassion.* The rest of the sermon is commentary on that statement. And we will ask, first, what authority there is for saying that a good church is conspicuous for goodness and compassion, and then ask what goodness and compassion may mean to you and me where we live today.

Last June a member of our church bought a book and sent it to me. I began reading this book in the last week in June, reading about ten pages every morning before breakfast and coming to the end of the 672 pages in the second week of September. I intended then to put it aside for a while, but to my own surprise, the next morning I picked up the book and started all over again. It will not, I hope sound like a bombast if I say that I think I shall never be quite the same again. The title of the book is one word: *Jesus*. The author is a Dutch Catholic named Edward Schillebeeckx Edward Schillebeeckx is now 67 years old, and the book may be considered the product of a lifetime of study and experience. It should be added, however, that his own thinking is heavily indebted to the best Christian scholarship for the past one hundred years.

The book set out to answer this question, putting the question in my own words: How and why was it that this indubitably historical human being, Jesus of Nazareth, came to be accepted as the Christ, that is, as the key to the ultimate reality we call God? To answer that question requires more than piety and faith; it requires penetrating back through many layers of history and tradition into Jewish life as it was in the time of Jesus. It demands the most careful kind of Bible reading, as well as study of sources outside the Bible. That is why I could absorb no more than about ten pages at a sitting. The purpose of Edward Schillebeeckx is not merely to get some historical facts straight; his passionate purpose is to find for himself and for his readers a living faith for today.

Among all the things one can say about this Jesus of Nazareth, I lift up this morning one characteristic. In Schillebeeckx's words, Jesus was "conspicuous for this goodness and compassion." That is the first and central impression he made: He was just plain good and extraordinarily compassionate with anyone in any kind of need. Would you like a definition of goodness? Here is one that I think will stand up: Goodness is not measured by what you don't do. Goodness is measured by the degree to which your self reaches out in compassion and helpfulness to other selves.

The *Book of Acts* gives us some samples of the earliest Christian preaching. As we heard in this morning's Scripture reading, one preacher, speaking of Jesus, talked about "how he went about doing good and healing all that are oppressed." The Gospel records are full of stories of men and women coming to him for help. That he did help many, healing some of what appeared to be physical ailments and others of spiritual maladies—of that there can be no doubt. Here was no person of merely genial goodwill; healing and liberation were his sole business. He was not interested in being a miracle-worker or in exhibiting his credentials as a prophet. His healing was in response to human need, nothing else. This was goodness in action.

Should we say that he was "selfless?" That does not seem to be the right word, for he had a very strong self. Let us say, rather, that this was a self that *existed* for others. The real miracle was not in this or that unusual thing he did. The miracle was that goodness, as good as that, could be in a human life. Before such purity of goodness, you and I can only bow in a mixture of awe and love—you and I who can try, only try, to get some of that goodness into our own lives.

If there were someone in the church this morning who had never heard of this Jesus, such a person might think I am making this up, inventing an ideal person. I am not inventing anything. Read the records with the care they deserve —and see!

Where did he get this kind of goodness and the courage to be that good? He was, he insisted, doing the will of his Father. To his Father-God he would be completely true. He used a special name for the God who was so intimately a part of him, calling God

Abba. This was a Jewish family word, almost as if one would say "Daddy." As he said, hours before he died, but said with his whole life, "Not my will but thy will be done." There is no explaining this Jesus without taking account of a supreme and commanding loyalty to God: To God, therefore to God's family, his life was a pledge of allegiance.

Therefore, some begin to say, especially after his death, that this human person was a true reflection of God. *Therefore*, they gave him the Jewish title Messiah, which in the Greek language was translated "Christos." *Therefore,* overwhelmed and changed by such goodness, they called him Savior and Lord. To the degree to which you and I get that goodness in our lives, he is our Savior.

As the days and months went by, he said that his kind of life would in some elicit loyalty and love and in others provoke hostility. For those who thought they were good enough because they broke no law, this kind of goodness was too much; they couldn't take it. In their panic at seeing their goodness exposed as specious, they made him out to be a criminal. He foresaw that this would happen and predicted his death at their hands. Did he turn back, decide to play safe? He couldn't! The God within him would not let him think of his own survival. How can we, so concerned about our "security," we who say self-preservation is the first law of life, how can we comprehend this man—this man for whom faithfulness, not security, was what mattered? So he went to his death, some of his own people turning him over to the Romans who inflicted on him their kind of horrible capital punishment.

And then? This kind of goodness, some decided, could not be dead. Whatever happened to his body, he was *alive*. There was no scientific proof of his being alive. There is reference to an empty tomb, but it was no empty tomb that convinced them. They could not entertain the idea that such a one could be put out of business by Roman soldiers. He had to be alive forevermore. And we are here today because this man, Jesus of Nazareth, was good with a goodness that, more than anything or anyone else, helps us to believe in a good God.

Our aim in this church is to have a Christlike church, isn't it? It must be, else why should we call ourselves Christians? Else our worship services are a "mere theological decoration of the world as it is." And being a Christlike church would mean being a church conspicuous for goodness and compassion. How could we manage that? Having many members is fine, but a large membership proves nothing. It is good to have a beautiful place of worship. I love this space in which we meet for worship. But a beautiful church does not guarantee being Christian. We have thrilling music from organ, choir, handbells, and who does not appreciate that? But great music is not enough to give us the reputation a church should have. Is the First Congregational Church, wherever its existence is known, conspicuous for its goodness and compassion? Is not this the reputation we should covet?

Some ways of being good are fairly simple, even if not always easy. Being sympathetic and helpful to members of one's family, to members of the church, to immediate friends and neighbors is important and good. But that does not cost much, only a little sensitivity that any serious person can manage. Giving money to lighten the burden of poverty in Port Chester, Stamford, Bridgeport is an exercise in Christian goodness. It is also as simple as writing a check.

Being good and compassionate in the educational system, in the legal profession, in medicine, in the business world, in domestic and international politics is a bit more complicated. One thing seems certain: Unless you can bring your sociology and your politics within speaking distance of your theology, your theology will not amount to much. How are goodness and compassion to be expressed in a corporation, in our American relations with the Soviet Union, with respect to our terrible, wasteful race to possess the most effective instruments of destruction? That requires some pretty rigorous thinking. I am very happy that we are to have three special public meetings in our church on that last question, meetings under the excellent theme, "Call to Faithfulness." And I hope many will come to the third meeting, as well as to the first two, because there we are to consider what faithfulness to Jesus Christ may mean in this tangled and dangerous international situation.

This is stewardship month in our church. How do we decide how much to give to the church and to other helping agencies? It could be helpful to aim at ten percent, just so we don't think tithing is going to win special favors from God. I think we should decide how much to give on the basis of a simple fact: You and I owe something; we owe a lot. We would not have a red cent without the help of others and of our whole society. And why should anyone put money into the treasury of this church? Is it not for the purpose of making the First Congregational Church conspicuous for goodness and compassion?

WHAT DOES IT MEAN TO BELIEVE IN GOD?

Sermon by the Rev. Dr. Herman F. Reissig
October 9, 1983

The year was 1929. The place, just behind the last pew in a church in Bridgeport. Most of those who had attended the morning's service had gone home. A few of us stood around talking. One of those who lingered was Jonathan Brierley, a real New England Yankee, owner of a small but prosperous business, unfailingly present whenever his church was open for worship. Jonathan Brierley had a question. What triggered the question I do not remember. Perhaps someone had, to his taste, spoken a little too positively about faith in God. With what sounded like a touch of impatience, J. B. said, "What does it mean to believe in God, anyway?"

Some weeks later, the question stuck in my mind, I went into the pulpit and offered some answers to the question. There is no hard evidence that the sermon caused a seismic spiritual upheaval in the church. On the suggestion of a church member, and through his generosity, it was printed in a little booklet and a few years later it was included in a book of sermons.

Both the booklet and the book have disappeared from my library. In any case, I would not have used that sermon this morning, partly because both the secular world and the theological world have changed since 1929, and partly because at eighty-four I know less than I knew at thirty.

Some of you may feel more comfortable during the first part of the sermon if you know in advance that the more affirmative words will come last. To achieve a truly inward faith in our time it is necessary first to get past some conceptions of God and faith in God that are not meaningful to the modern mind.

Last Sunday, our Minister of Music, Richard Vogt, told the congregation that we are soon to have a new supplementary collection of hymns. Why are we doing this? Surely not because our committees on worship and on music have an itch for novelty. Throughout the Christian world new hymns are being written and assembled because of a perception that many of the verbal images in the old hymns are no longer good channels for conveying the water that gives life. They are loved as we love antique chairs; graceful and familiar, but not good pieces for everyday use.

The birth of new hymns is only one part of the story. The whole theological world is in ferment. No, "ferment" is too weak. The world of theological thinking is boiling. In seminary and university, to some extent in local churches, a question is being asked: *How can we talk about God in our time?* What is so different about our time and when did "our time" begin? It started about three hundred years ago with the scientific revolution, followed by its offspring, technology, and what we now call high technology. These have caused a profound change in our thinking about the universe, human life, and God. We are only just now, in the latter years of this century, beginning to feel the full force of this revolution.

One of the best ways to describe our contemporary situation is in some words of the Christian martyr, Dietrich Bonhoeffer. In prison, from which he was taken to be hanged by the nazi tyrant, Dietrich Bonhoeffer wrote hundreds of letters, which were smuggled out. In these letters, Bonhoeffer used a phrase that has become famous. He said, "Modern man has come of age." It may sound like a bumptious, strutting assertion. Not so for Bonhoeffer, who was a man of prayer and incessantly studied his Bible. To say that human beings have now "come of age" means that in a way not possible before the scientific and technological revolutions, we human beings are doing for ourselves what earlier people prayed God to do. Somewhat as a young adult takes charge of his or her own life, human beings are taking charge of themselves and their worlds.

One illustration can stand for something pervasive and universal. The Nobel Laureate biologist Peter Medawar and his wife write in a book just published: "For a long time the transplantation of organs—particularly the heart—was frowned upon by public figures who arrogated to themselves the responsibility for being the conscience of the world and the spokesmen of a God-fearing, right-thinking minority. These people regarded transplantation as undignified and pleaded instead for natural death. So deep-seated, however, is the human preference for being alive that these spokesmen have not carried their point." From irrigating instead of praying for rain, to central heating and air conditioning, to defiance of gravity with airplanes, to replacing diseased human organs, on to genetic engineering, modern human beings instead of asking God to do something are doing it, or trying to do it themselves. The fear that if we undertake too much we will, like the people in the Tower of Babel story, be put to confusion, has died out. There is in modern people a deep resolve to take charge.

In this new situation we can make serious mistakes as, for example, in pollution of air and water in our rush to create more goods and energy. We can do radical damage to the balance of nature. We call this playing God which can be mighty risky. Nevertheless, once we know how to do something that we think will be useful, we are going to do it.

If, now, human beings are taking charge, what does this mean for belief in God, for prayer, for our public worship? My friends of First Church, there is no use trying to evade this question. We have to face it and try to think through it. At this point I may get a little ahead of my argument by saying that if you and I have any faith at all we shall not be afraid. Surely we do not wish to be like the minister who said to me many years ago when I raised a question about a certain belief, "I never," he said, "read anything except my Bible. I am afraid of anything that might disturb my faith." What a pitifully weak kind of faith that man had!

Let us now identify some conceptions of God and faith in God that we must give up if we want to find an internal and living faith. (I don't enjoy even the appearance of being negative, but there is that famous epigram of Ralph Waldo Emerson, "When the half-gods go, the gods arrive.")

It is not possible for a thoughtful person today to believe in a God who dwells in some heaven apart from this world; who created in specific and separate actions all the billions of forms of existence of which we are now aware; who personally and specifically wills that this baby shall be born and that person die; who has a blueprint for every human life; who wills nations into being and deliberately destroys empires; who "keeps books" on everything I do from morning to night; who rewards with prosperity those who say they believe in him and is angry with atheists; who sends lovely weather but also tornados and earthquakes; who decrees that this child shall be born with a good working brain and that child be born retarded or imbecilic, that one soldier shall come home from war alive and well while another's body shall come home in a casket.

Theoretically, one could perhaps believe in the existence of such a deity. But as soon as you stop to think you are in trouble. For if God has a detailed plan for your life, what about the six million Jews, including one million children, who died by gun, poison and fire in the extermination camps of the Holocaust? And here is something I read in a newspaper some years ago: A man went to an airport but missed his plane, by minutes. That plane crashed, killing everyone on board. The man said to a newspaper reporter, "God was good to me." Indeed! His words sound pious and believing, and one understands that he would be relieved and thankful. But are we really going to think God singled him out to live, while deciding the others should perish? Name your accidental deaths, your victims of cancer, your millions who live in misery; you are not willing, are you, to say all this is according to divine plan?

To be sure, we have to be careful here. For the word "God," almost by definition, means power and an intelligence beyond our human fathoming. As the Psalmist wrote, "My ways are not your ways and my thoughts are not your thoughts, saith the Lord." Who am I, a terribly limited mortal, to set bounds to God? Still, how could we believe in, much less love, a being who offends our best human thinking and our most humane impulses?

That "almighty King," that monarchical Ruler of all things in heaven and in earth, that "unmoved Mover" that earlier theologians pictured, that giver of direct rewards to some and of pain to others; that Supreme Being who is supposed to be the Great Lover, but expects us to beg and beg before he will bestow his blessing—No, if we insist on some such picture of God, our churches may thrive as social centers, but with only a vaporous something called "God."

So what is left? If what I have said is valid—and I should emphasize here that I have not been expressing a merely private, individualistic view but the view of increasing numbers of responsible, conscientious people—if what I have said is valid, how shall we think of God and belief in God?

I said earlier that the theological world is boiling. Serious black theologians reject the white God, but not God. Women theologians, such as Rosemary Reuther, reject the masculine God, but not God. Latin American Christians, living under crippling oppression, think of God mainly as the Great Liberator. Some have found help in meditation learned from Buddhism. Some scientists find in universal natural law evidence of Mind at the beginning and at the center of things. Others find help in what is know as Process Theology: God, like human life, is not static but in process. The key words are "development" and "becoming."

One of the phenomena that impresses me is the human brain. What a stunning, breathtaking organ the brain is! A biologist can take it apart, name its constituent parts, tell us that logical reasoning comes from one part of the brain while poetry and romance come from another part. But explain it? Explain how electrical impulses coming in through eye, ear or fingers jump from tissue to tissue and come out as a symphony by Beethoven, a play by Shakespeare, or a love letter from Jack to Jane? No one can explain that? How did such a thing come to pass? Did a superhuman being plan and make this incredibly intricate organ? Hard to imagine. Did it just happen, certain chemicals coming together by pure accident over millions of years? Even harder to believe.

If the believer has some explaining to do, the materialist has at least as much explaining to do. And, there is the problem of evil. Yes, there is evil here, massive, terrible evil. Look at us! In an insane race to get the most instruments for killing. That alone is enough to tempt one to moral cynicism. Look at the fighting in Lebanon, in Central America, in Chad, the brutal suppression of the black majority in South Africa, look at the suppression of men like Sakharov in the Soviet Union, or people in the United States rolling in luxury while American babies are seriously undernourished.

And yet, there is goodness, there is beauty, there is love, there is helpfulness, there is some moral progress, and there is undying hope. If I could just ally myself with the struggle for justice, for bridge-building instead of gunmaking, for creating a true human family instead of racism and chauvinistic nationalism, would I then be practicing faith in God? I think so.

My God is no off-earth potentate, making rules, alternately sweet and harsh. My God suffers with us, feels our agony, dies on a cross, languishes in prisons, weeps at hospital beds. My God lures, invites, pulls and pushes – and, being God, does not give up. Will God win? We human beings could defeat him on this earth – defeat him with atomic weapons. Then God might begin over again, on this earth or on another planet. But I join with the millions who don't want all that we have built and achieved turned into poisoned ashes through human folly, and therefore I join with the millions crying, "Stop this insane notion that you are going to save with atomic weapons anything worth saving!"

My God does not ask for praise. We don't think highly of those who are always looking for compliments. To praise is good for us, for as the poet said, "We needs must love (and praise) the highest when we see it." But God's desire must be that we do justice and love mercy and help one another. My God wants us to align ourselves with a moving toward justice and mutual aid. My God is a great magnet that keeps drawing me back toward his purposes, especially when I want to enjoy myself and let the world go hang.

I call myself a Christian, not because I am good, which I am not, any more than you are. I call myself a Christian because that man Jesus of Nazareth is for me the local presence of God, the one kind of God I can believe in. Believing in God means betting your life that God is like that, and then, however much you may slip and fall, always letting the Great Magnet draw you back to him.

My God is the God of the Cross and of unending resurrection.

The Choir sings: "O Love that wilt not let me go..."

The Benediction: Now may the magnet that is love and beauty and goodness draw you and hold you, giving you sure ground to stand on and faith to live by.

SINGING THE LORD'S SONG IN A FOREIGN LAND

Sermon by the Rev. Dr. Herman F. Reissig

May 6, 1984

For a start on this sermon, let us see if we can make an old story from the East come alive for us in the United States in the year 1984. The Hebrew people began their life as a nation with exodus from Egypt. Thereafter, the word "deliverance," what we today like to call liberation, was a central word in their life. After centuries of struggle and fighting, they had their days of glory under Kings Solomon and David.

In the story we are looking at, they had been conquered by Babylon, their magnificent temple razed to the ground, and many of the people carried off as slaves. In their misery, one of their number, whose name has been lost, wrote a poem that we know as the 137th psalm. Let us listen to this cry of sorrow, of lively remembrance, ending in a terrible cry for vengeance:

By the waters of Babylon,
there we sat down and wept
when we remembered Zion.
On the willows there
we hung up our lyres.
For there our captors
required of us song,
And our tormentors, mirth, saying
"Sing unto us one of the songs of Zion."
How shall we sing the Lord's song
in a foreign land?
If I forget you, O Jerusalem,
let my right hand wither.
Let my tongue cleave to the roof of my mouth
if I do not remember you,
If I do not set Jerusalem
above my highest joy!
Remember, O Lord, against the Edomites
the day of Jerusalem,

How they said, "Raze it, raze it!
down to its foundations!"
O daughter of Babylon, you devastator!
Happy shall he be who requites you
with what you have done to us!
Happy shall he be who takes your little ones
and dashes them against the rock!

If your imagination is in good working order, you will have no difficulty picturing the scene: a crowd of desperately homesick exiles, not left alone in their grief but urged to sing "Go ahead, sing for us one of the songs you used to sing back in Jerusalem. Entertain us!" To which they reply, in their poet's words, "How can we sing the Lord's song in this foreign land?" They cannot adjust to this. The thought of the homeland produces tears, not songs.

But then, a solemn vow: Jerusalem, we will not forget! We will keep the blessed place in our hearts and never stop hoping for return. One might wish the psalm ended there. But the Bible is an honest book and does not suppress the worst. Human beings are capable of terrible cruelty, especially if they have been badly misused, or if they are scared. The exiles demand vengeance. Centuries later, a young Jew wanted people to stop returning evil for evil and, instead, return good for evil, which is one reason for calling him Savior. But we human beings can hardly ever manage that.

Moslems, especially Palestinian Moslems, want to drive Israelis into the sea to drown, old people, babies and all. Irish Catholics murder Irish Protestants. The family and friend of a murdered person gather around a courthouse and shout for the death of the murderer. Russians have a mountain of weapons for killing Americans, and Americans have enough warheads to kill all the Russians seven times over. Repay evil with good? Let's have none of such dovish talk! Answer threat with threat; match gun for gun. If your enemy plans evil, plan worse evil against him. Peace through words of peace? The conventional wisdom says, "Peace through strength"—military strength.

I spare you the statistics of warheads, and their destructive power; of nuclear submarines and their load of death; of bombers and missile emplacements in the ground. You can read the numbers and weights and the speed of delivery: so many on our side, so many on the other side, until, reading, you are dizzy. For two decades the United States was ahead. After the Cuban missile crisis, Russia decided to catch up, and by 1980 was considered by some to be forging ahead of us. We then began a mighty campaign to catch up with them. They had their SS20 missiles in Eastern Europe pointed at our allies; we started placing our Pershing missiles in Germany pointed at them.

The negotiators, who sat for months around a table counting and comparing and getting nowhere, have gone home. Stalemate—while on each side the scientists, technologists, the Pentagon and Kremlin military planners work feverishly to create additional instruments of death to use or to put on some future bargaining table. Claims and counterclaims. They, our President says, are the "locus of evil" in the world. We, they insist, are planning a first strike. The speech writers on both sides, one suspects, rack their brains for the most damning nouns and the ugliest adjectives. Both sides fill the skies with cameras that take pictures of all but the tiniest objects, and both sides put their spies and counterspies wherever they can seduce and suborn and sneak them in.

We call this realism. We call it defense, provision for security, protection of our way of life, patriotism. On both sides money badly needed for food, medicine, housing, decaying cities and crumbling roads goes for more weapons. On both sides there is agreement that this is regrettable, but if we skimp on defense enemy may blackmail us into submission. "Too bad, but we have to take the world the way it is."

So we dehumanize each other until we in their eyes and they in our eyes are no longer fathers and mothers who love their children, and young people who want to grow up with a chance for work and play! We count the weapons as if they were not designed to reduce homes, libraries, and places of business to rubble, and rip human flesh to shreds! The arms race has become an inhuman game. I would not wish to be an arms control negotiator on either side. For, so it seems to me, the negotiator must be cold as ice, all human feeling kept out of his mind while he counts and measures bullets and bombs.

But I speak this morning to Americans; there are probably no Russians in the congregation. There is, therefore, no point in admonishing *them*. We, in this church, call ourselves Christians. In our churches we sing the Lord's song. The words of the Lord's song are peace, goodwill, justice, love, forgiveness, mutual helpfulness, even love of our enemies.

Then we go out into the everyday world and find the kind of world I have been describing. The question is: Can we sing the Lord's song in this Babylon? Can we sing it anywhere except in church and perhaps in our homes and between dear friends? Before I go on to suggest ways in which we can sing the Lord's song in Babylon, let me deal with a possible objection.

There may be someone in the congregation who wants to interrupt the sermon and say, "Now, wait a minute! Are you implying there is no moral difference between the United States and Russia?" My answer is, no, between our two societies there is a vast difference. Neither we nor they are as good as we like to claim, but between us there are wide, deep differences. On the one side, no *habeas corpus*, no independent judiciary, no right to criticize government policies, no real freedom of religion, no freedom to parade or strike or to vote leaders out of or into office, no right to leave the country, no right to travel within the country without a properly-stamped internal passport.

On our side, glaring, even sickening, failures to live up to our ideas, but still an almost unhindered right to protest, an almost unlimited right to vote, a free press, an almost free pulpit, the freedom of the pulpit being only restricted by pressure from the pew and the unChristlike timidity of many preachers. For many Americans, especially black young people, there is no freedom to work; no work is available to them. For many Americans there is little freedom of opportunity; they have grown up in a crushing poverty-culture. Still, as human societies go, we are free to change and improve and dissent and move around. No government can tell the churches what they may or may not say, as leaders in the Washington administration discovered when they tried to get our

Catholic bishops to say what the administration wanted them to say. No, like all the rest of you, the one preaching here today will not pretend that our way is morally better than their way.

Nevertheless, we Americans do share with the Russians responsibility for this wretched, menacing arms race. Before telling you what one Christian tries to do about it, let us go back for a moment to what, according to their poet, the Hebrews would *not* do. They vowed not to forget Jerusalem and the songs of Zion. This is where you and I in this church should start: with what they called Zion and we call Christ. This is the place from which, if we are serious Christians, we orient ourselves. A Christian is a person who, no matter where he/she is, never forgets Christ and his way. The President says . . . the Pentagon says . . . We will listen, but Christians march to the sound of a different drum. If you and I do not intend, in public as well as in private matters, to take Jesus of Nazareth seriously, it would be better to be honest and stop going to church. Clearly what we Americans are doing today in many areas, but especially in the arms race, is not Christ's way. No Christian should feel at home in this kind of world. Like those ancient Hebrews in Babylon, we are exiles. Or, if you think the word "exile" is too strong, we must at least feel the tension, an almost agonizing tension, between our religion and the way our world thinks and acts. Translate the old poet's words like this: If I do not remember Christ, may my Christian words stick in my throat.

The rest of the sermon will be one Christian's testimony. I intend no prescription for you who are listening, although I hope some of you will agree.

First, like Martin Luther King, I have a dream for my country. The dream will not become a reality, at least not in the foreseeable future. Nevertheless, it is a good dream and one I am not going to give up. The dream goes like this: The United States makes two decisions; it will stop inventing and making instruments for destruction and killing, and it will do this without prior assurance that other nations will do likewise. That's the negative part of the dream, not by itself enough.

Then, at the same time, this great country goes into positive action. It pours its technological genius, its administrative ability and its wealth into lifting its own people and helping to lift other peoples out of poverty and deprivation. Our conscious and specific national goal is the well-being and happiness of women, men, and children wherever they live. We set an example of justice and mercy for all to see. The victims of avoidable sickness, the victims of racial suppression, the victims of crushing poverty, the people deprived of elementary human rights in the United States, in Asia, in Africa, in Europe, in Latin America, hear of this and are glad. With one accord they sing, "God Bless America." They say, "This is the leadership we have been waiting for. Now at last we are offered – not guns, but food; not bombers, but homes; not missiles, but medicine; and not submission, but freedom."

In my dream, some individuals, some groups, some nations will exult, "Ha! Now we have got those Americans where we want them. They have voted for weakness and we, the strong, can take over." But from around the world, from the little people, the hungry, the people of goodwill, the vast majority, there goes up such a cry of support for this new America that those who still lust for power will be isolated; they will have no support. They therefore will be compelled to imitate the new America —forced to keep up with America in helping and saving.

So runs my dream. It might just work. Yes, it might work. Or it might not. There was one, long ago, who, listening only to His God, did nothing but good. It didn't work. Scornfully and in brutal fashion they got rid of him. But God fooled the powers of darkness. This man *lives* while the iron fists and the swordsmen are unwept, unhonored and unsung. On bended knee we praise *him* as "the" last, best hope of earth."

But the dream will not, in our time, become a reality. The risk will not be taken. So what's left? What actual steps can you and I take—steps toward breaking our bondage to the arms race?

Here are some of the things that you and I can do, beginning today:

- We can try to understand some things about the Russians: that they like ourselves are afraid; afraid of war, afraid of being invaded and conquered. We can recognize that if the that if the Russians are moved by a messianic nationalism, so are many Americans. We can utterly reject the claim that Russia is "the locus of evil" in our insisting instead that the locus of evil is in the old human tendency of the strong to keep their power at whatever cost to others.

- We can see with complete clarity that nothing worth saving can be saved in a war fought with nuclear weapons and also that there is no decency in "deterrence" if deterrence means, as it does mean, that we plan to reduce so many cities to ash heaps and so many lives to radiated dust.
- We can insist that our government put less emphasis on armaments and more, far more, on rational, peaceful ways of dealing with international differences. Having army, air force and naval academies, and seeing that our Department of State, supposedly our peace department, is not free to differ from President and Pentagon, we can support the creation of a Peace Academy in which free men and women will work full time to search out and refine ways to build a more peaceful world.
- We can write letters, join in mass protests, attend meetings on peace, sign petitions, march in peace parades, support the "freeze," send checks to those candidates for political office who seem to stand most clearly for negotiation and reconciliation, who "stand tall," not because America is well armed, but because America stands for justice and human well-being. We can recognize that the impulse toward national self-righteousness afflicts every nation and especially the strongest nations and, if we cannot modify the self-righteousness of other nations, we can guard against that danger in our own nation.
- We can say "no" to the hawks and join the doves, and not be intimidated when we are called unrealistic, naive, or unpatriotic. In such ways, and in many other ways, we can sing the Lord's song in a foreign land.

New York Herald Tribune
Photogravure Section

Herman Reissig's influence in his earlier years was apparent as he spoke to a group of 2500 undergraduates at Columbia University as part of a national demonstration for peace on April 26, 1936.

APPENDIX II

INTRODUCTION TO EXCERPTS FROM *MAN'S NEW HOME*

Man's New Home, Herman Reissig's only book, was published in 1964 when he was age 65.

In the *Introduction*, Herman explains that "the world is viewed as man's home" and that "we should be grateful for our God-given home, making it as good for man as we can manage," at a time when "man is changing almost every aspect of his home." He concludes the *Introduction* with these paragraphs:

> This book was written in a mood of sympathy for liberals, conservatives, the confused, the contentious, Republicans, Democrats, young people, older people—all of us. All of us are together in a world whose changes and events are beyond our understanding or mastery. Even with those whose views we reject, we must try to keep a bond of sympathy and understanding. If we must use labels to designate groups and movements, we can at least strive to avoid the name-calling that is usually both a substitute for thinking and a symptom of self-righteousness.
>
> Without supposing that I see very far or with exceptional clarity, I want to present in this book some aspects of our terrible and wonderful contemporary world as I see them, in the hope that some who read will find at least a measure of insight and of guidance for action.

Although the book was written almost thirty years ago, there is much that is still relevant and useful. We have chosen three sections that we believe are particularly timeless in their message:

- **The Meaning of Sin**
- **The Necessity of Force and The Way of the Cross**
- **The Roots of Christian Social Action**

Herman concludes the last of these three sections, which is the final chapter of *Man's New Home,* with this paragraph:

* * *

> In brief, Christian social action is Christian love of the neighbor – love that knows *what* a man is, serves him *where* he is, and is resolved that the social order and all its institutions shall contribute to his fulfillment.

THE MEANING OF SIN

Excerpt from Chapter One of *Man's New Home*

In speaking of the human person we have said that he has, according to our faith, an infinite worth. But the same religion insists that man is a sinner. Next to the denial of man's worth, the denial that he is a sinful being has been the greatest obstacle to the successful handling of social problems.

If we do not believe that every human being is infinitely worthful, we move logically toward such results as racism, Nazism (including genocide), or toward the worst manifestations of communism. If we say we believe in the worth of the individual person but do not keep this belief in the center of our thinking about social problems, we get slums, racial discrimination, and pursuit of power and wealth for their own sake, all of which are so prevalent in democratic "Christian" societies.

If, on the other hand, we do not understand that man is by nature sinful, or if we fail to keep that fact in mind, we get personal self-righteousness, national self-righteousness, class self-righteousness, intolerance, bigotry, fanatical utopianism, and a host of other evils. From the Marxist, who has no use for the idea of sin because he thinks evil is merely the concomitant of "the class society," to the American Christian who doesn't like "all this talk about sin," the wages of not understanding the fact and nature of sin is a kind of death. If I, who write this book, forget that I am by nature sinful, there will not be much chance of my writing a useful book. If you, the reader, do not take account of what sin does to your thinking, you may reject even what is true in it.

Sin is not a pleasant word, but no one has been able to think of a pleasanter word to designate the condition. What is the condition? If we say it is that in man which makes it impossible for him to be an impartial observer in any matter involving his personal interests, we have covered most of the meaning of sin. Man's sinfulness means, in other words, an ineradicable subjectivity, so deep and pervasive as to make objectivity unattainable except in some areas of scientific investigation and technological work.

The scientist in his laboratory may approach complete objectivity. That is, his personal interests are not permitted to get in the way of seeing facts. Even here, the scientist's desire to be the first to announce a discovery or to gain prestige for his university may somewhat influence the quality of his work. A mechanic investigating the malfunctioning of my automobile engine may seem to be a model of objectivity, unless his personal interest in making as much profit as possible leads him to find more trouble than is actually present!

But when we are in the areas of personal relations, family life, domestic social policy, or international affairs, the thinking of every last one of us is to a greater or lesser degree influenced by our personal or group interest. The ego hovers around the edges when it is not at the very center of our thinking. No matter how we try, we cannot avoid being influenced by our particular background and training as well as our unconscious desire for attention, prestige, security, power and profit.

Consider two illustrations, one from domestic affairs and one from international relations. The publisher of a newspaper insists on the right of the people to know what government officials are doing. This is commendable. Newspaper publishers and reporters are among our indispensable champions of the freedom to learn and to speak. It is their duty to push open doors that public officers would often like to keep closed. But how nice for the newspapers! They can almost always make themselves believe that what is in their interests as commercial enterprises is also in the interests of the general public. The reporter can pose as a disinterested champion of the freedom of the press even when, as often happens, he is trying to beat another reporter to a scoop or is trying to get information that an objective view of the public interest would consider better not to publish. Being a sinful man, the reporter is often quite unable to distinguish his personal interest from the public interest. Someone not in the newspaper business is needed to point out the possible bias.

So, in similar fashion, the clergyman, the businessman, the politician, and the physician, all being of a sinful nature, can never be sure to what extent each is looking objectively at the facts and the public welfare and to what extent each is unconsciously looking out for his private interests.

What is it in the relations between nations that almost always convinces the American, the Frenchman, or the Russian that the policy of his own nation is so obviously right that only some perversity in the others prevents them from seeing it? Call it bias or prejudice, call it anything we like, it is a fact of life. And it is a lamentable disability that makes all human relations difficult and which, unrecognized, often makes controversy acrimonious and unproductive.

Paul Tillich, Christian theologian, is right when he says the word *sin* should never be used in its plural form. For sin is not this or that specific thought or action; sin is a condition—a universal condition. It is a condition of human nature that puts the self in the center of things, that asserts the self against men and against God, that mixes up the best of men.

The Christian gospel has a partial remedy. It says that if a man can be brought to confess this human disability, recognizing his ineradicable egoism, he will have by that very fact some guard against it. To put it in theological terms, God cannot forgive us (release us from its power) if we do not honestly confess it. But honest confession automatically brings forgiveness (release) because then we say to ourselves, "Oh, oh! I'd better watch my step! I simply cannot be as righteous and unselfish as I was about to pretend."

Let us see how this works in practice. Suppose that several Christians are discussing a controversial political issue. The debate waxes hot. Tempers begin to rise. Some accuse their opponents of ignorance or bias or selfishness or partisan politics, or reactionism, or leftist sympathies, or arrogance. Suppose then that one member of the group recalls the Christian teaching about sin and forgiveness. Suppose he should stand up and say to those with whom he is contending something like this: "Look! I feel sure that I am right about this matter and that you are mistaken. But I am a sinful man. I am not God, knowing truth from error and right from wrong with absolute clarity. When I do the best I can, I can still be wrong. I would like to think I have reached my position by a process of pure reasoning. But since I am a human being, this obviously cannot be so. Even a psychologist would have a hard time bringing all my motives to light. If you cannot agree with my position, will you please, nevertheless, forgive me and give me your hand? You also, my opponent, are a sinner. You, no more than I, comprehend your motives. You, no more than I, are free of unrecognized prejudices. I, therefore, forgive you and give you my hand. Let us, having confessed our pathetic sinfulness and having forgiven each other, proceed with our discussion. And may God accept our sincerity and forgive our frailty!"

It might be added, as a footnote, that this approach will not always work. In a long discussion with a chance acquaintance, I tried to be honest about my own biases. But she absolutely refused to admit that she had any. Her opinions, which seemed to me an example of almost pure prejudice, seemed to her the inevitable conclusions of pure reason. Perhaps she felt that in the very act of confessing awareness of my own bias, I was really saying, "See how objective I am!" The pitfalls provided by sin are too numerous. It is never easier to agree with the apostle Paul than when he groans, "Wretched man that I am! Who will deliver me from this body of death?"

Fortunately, we have in democratic societies social devices that save us from the worst effects of our egoism. The industrialist's defects of vision are partly compensated by the different vision of the labor union, and vice versa. The politician's one-sided tendencies are checked by a watchful and wary public. The progressive is fortunately unable to have the whole show to himself, being forced to make room for the conservative. The average citizen is saved from some of the results of his egoistic impulses by the law and by public disapproval. This is the system of what has been called "countervailing forces."

In international affairs, let us be grateful that no nation, including our own, can always prevail. On this point no comment I can make could be more to the point than some words spoken by Edmund Burke in 1795 when Great Britain was engaged in war against Napoleon. Incidentally Burke confused liberal political goals with personal ambition in hopeless fashion. He said:

"Among precautions against ambition, it may not be amiss to take one precaution against our own. I must fairly say I dread our own power and our own ambition. I dread our being too much dreaded. It is ridiculous to say that we are not men and that as men we shall never wish to aggrandize ourselves in one way or another . . . We are already in possession of almost all the commerce in the world. Our empire in India is an awful thing. If we should come to be in a condition not only to have all this ascendancy in commerce, but to be absolutely able, without the least control, to hold the commerce of all nations totally dependent upon our good pleasure, we may say that we shall not abuse this astonishing and unheard of power. But every other nation will think we shall abuse it. It is impossible but that, sooner or later, this state of things must produce a combination against us which may end in our ruin."

Politics in the 20th Century, Morgenthau

THE NECESSITY OF FORCE AND THE WAY OF THE CROSS

Excerpts from Chapter Five of *Man's New Home*

The Necessity of Force

Both clergymen and lay members of the churches often underrate the place of law and the use of force in the social structure. I once heard a missionary on furlough claim with a straight face that whereas governments in their dealings with other countries rely on force, Christian missions put sole dependence on "the spiritual." This sounds like earnest piety. Actually, one must conclude, it is a case of blindness to reality caused by the unconscious impulse to claim superiority for one's self and one's profession. Missionary work is made possible in part by minimum economic and political social structures, which are organized and maintained by governments that depend partly on force. The nation from which the missionary goes out is not constituted of purely spiritual forces. His very passport is a product of legal and police structure. And if there were no law at all in the country to which he goes, he would scarcely be able to preach the gospel.

"Law," it is often asserted, "cannot make people good." The assertion is made as an antidote to the "let's pass a law" mentality. But the denigration of the place of law is often the expression of a particular objection to particular laws. Law cannot make people inwardly good, but it is an indispensable tool in helping them to be better citizens than they could be without law. It would be a ludicrous conceit to claim that I am a more virtuous man than George Washington. But in at least one respect my social conduct is morally superior. I do not own slaves. Why do I not own slaves? Law has stepped in and said, "Thou shalt not!" Even today the moral sense does not universally support the freedom of the Negro. I might just possibly be able to prove to myself that a little slavery would be good for me and for the slaves. Fortunately, I am spared any tussle with my conscience on this matter by existence of the law.

No person is good enough or wise enough to be a good citizen without aid of law. And there will always be some who, unrestrained by law, will not even try to be good citizens. Obviously, we cannot wait for orderly social relations until everyone is superlatively wise and good. "That government governs best that governs least" is a favorite aphorism among those who are alarmed by the body of legislation that has given us the welfare state. This obviously cannot be taken literally, since consistent movement toward less government would bring us finally to no government. But those who first propounded the statement were not anarchists, nor are those who quote it today. In fact, the proponents of this doctrine will often be found advocating a new piece of legislation.

The question of desirable or undesirable extension of governmental jurisdiction cannot be answered by general principles in favor of or against new legislation. The real question is: At what point in the evolution of consensus on social goals does it seem wise or necessary to bring in government? Or, to put the question in less abstract terms: When does a concern for the welfare of persons, which should always be our central concern, require that law be used to protect and further their welfare? On this, citizens of equal intelligence and virtue may differ. Those who are inclined to rush to Washington, D.C. with every emerging social problem should spend more time considering whether local action, either voluntary or governmental, might not be preferable. The danger of overcentralization is not nonexistent. On the other hand, those who on principle fight against almost every extension of government fail to grasp the democratic conception of government as an instrument that the people can use and control for their benefit. They also fail to see that in modern industrialized, urbanized societies we must do more things together through government than was required in earlier times.

This discussion of law seems relevant here because law, with some exceptions, is not effective law unless there is provision for enforcement. All political societies rest upon two pillars: consent and coercion. Even dictatorships depend to a larger degree than is generally believed on voluntary agreement with their policies. In an established democracy there is more reliance on free consent. The law, made by the freely chosen representatives of the people, represents a wide consensus, and the policeman remains in the background. But the police power must usually be present. To adapt Pascal's aphorism, if power without justice is tyranny, justice without power is impotent. Even the goodness of the good and the wisdom of the wise cannot, without the policeman's coercion, maintain a tolerable order. This is neatly symbolized in a sign on one of the New Jersey State highways. The first sentence on the sign reads, "Please Do Not Discard Rubbish." The second sentence says, "Fifty Dollars Fine!" The threat is useful even for "nice" motorists whose niceness may be unequal to community requirements.

If force is indispensable in settled domestic societies, it should be clear that world order will also have to rely upon it. In relations between the nations, moral suasion is even less effective than in domestic matters within the nations. Far less! Christians will, of course, put heavy emphasis on creating understanding and goodwill. It is their primary function, in this area, to insist on our common humanity under God (not merely "one nation under God") and to inculcate the respect and concern for persons that so easily is pushed out of sight in all great social structures. Christians should see in Russia, in China, and in India the men, women and children whom God loves and whom they ought to love as neighbors. The first concern of Christians should be to strengthen the human bond. By preaching the gospel and in Christ's name serving human needs and by encouraging personal association across political and cultural barriers, they will seek to pull down the dividing walls.

This approach is fundamental and indispensable. But one of the weakness of Christians is that in their appropriate stress on understanding and goodwill, they are too indifferent to the indispensable functions of power in world affairs— power understood as the capability of a nation or an alliance or an international organization to impose its will upon others.

The Way of the Cross

What should Christians say to the plea that in its dealings with other nations, especially hostile nations, the United States should follow "the way of the cross?"

We should, I suggest, remind ourselves at the outset that in no other area of organized social life do we rely solely on suffering love. Here and there an individual person comes close to it. Seeing his fellowmen without the elemental necessities of life, he allows himself only as much food, clothing, and shelter as seems really necessary to sustain himself in health and efficiency. He turns away from everything that could be called self-indulgence. He seriously tries to meet anger with the soft answer that turns away wrath. His response to aggressive and unjust action is always an attempt to overcome evil with good. He rejects, as far as he can, every kind of physical coercion or violent action. If he is struck, he will not strike back. In an extreme situation, he will die rather than meet force with force. His guiding principle is reconciliation.

Such a life is deeply impressive. It stimulates the best in us and makes us at least a little ashamed of our selfishness and our angry ways. Mohandas K. Gandhi and Albert Schweitzer appeal deeply to us as examples of what seems a better way. The Freedom Riders and other groups, resolved on justice but equally resolved to refrain from violence, following the way of suffering love and loving the oppressor as well as the oppressed—such persons and groups by their example rebuke our belligerent contentiousness and our too easy reliance on force. I recall inviting to speak in one of the churches I served a man who tried as hard as anyone I have known or heard of to live by the Sermon on the Mount. When he had finished speaking, many in the congregation—a little bewildered, not sure it was "practical"—said with a shaking of the head, "He's got something there!"

Would not all of us like to be free of our brawling, egoistic ways? And do we not feel at least some inclination to test what sacrificial, reconciling love might accomplish? Yes, but at least two reservations must be made here. First, no one has the moral right to enjoin the United States government to follow "the way of the cross" in its relations with other nations unless he is making a serious effort to follow this way in his personal life. To put it bluntly, most Christian pacifists are not in a good position to exhort the Department of State or the Pentagon to adopt a "Christian foreign policy." When we begin to cast stones at the government because, as we say, it substitutes compromise and expediency for principle, we might if we listened hear a voice saying, "Let him who does not compromise cast the first stone."

Some of us, sincere and earnest as we may be, are in fact asking that foreign policy be purer than our personal policies. Loyalty to Christ must begin with me. Let me set an example! I shall soon find out how costly is the way of the cross. I shall soon discover also that what looks like a really Christian response to a situation may sometimes have injurious results—more injurious, perhaps, than the response of those who are content with more ambiguous ways of responding. By all means, let Christians press for the fullest possible use of reason, of acts of goodwill and mercy, of negotiation, of all instruments and methods that grow out of the desire to live and help live. Let there be no easy acquiescence in reliance on force. Let Christ on his cross make us acutely uneasy about the kind of power to which we too exclusively look for protection. International relations most certainly need a perpendicular judgment from a place far above our warring ways. Only let us not speak to the government as if we, in pulpit and pew, were ourselves on Golgotha!

In the second place, it is necessary to recognize that organized societies cannot dispense with force. The best we can do is keep force in its place, as a servant of love. The concept of force as a servant of love may strike some Christians as a gross discord. Actually, a love that will never in any situation use force is not love of human beings; it is love of love. It is love of a principle or a method instead of love for living persons. Will a parent not by physical force thrust his child away from a live electric wire? Would a verbal plea in this instance be more loving? Will love refrain from intervening with force if a neighbor is assaulted in vicious fashion? To say that Christian love requires withdrawal of police protection from a James Meredith on the campus of the University of Mississippi, in the certain knowledge that he would be beaten and perhaps killed, would be a strange conception of love. It seems clear that force sometimes has the sanction of love.

Perhaps our trouble at this point arises from thinking of love primarily as a method or means. But love has no meaning apart from persons. Love is a passionate attachment to the worth and dignity of the person. It is not an instrument; it is a relationship. Loving the actual person—this man, that woman, this child—earnestly wanting the best for him, I then ask myself how I can best serve him. I can do this in many varied ways, all of them in response to love. He is lonely: I give him friendship. He is hungry: I give him food. He is poisoned by resentments: I try to help him clear his mind of the perilous stuff. He is ignorant: I help provide education. He is an alcoholic or a drug addict or a compulsive gambler: I try to make cure available, and also pay attention to the social conditions that put too much strain on his character.

But the persons that I love as a Christian have another category of needs. They need an orderly society: a society in which the strong and the ruthless cannot with impunity hurt their neighbors, and in which public services are reasonably well provided. Minorities in the society had protection against majorities, and majorities against ruthless minorities. The persons constituting a nation need protection against the destruction of their homes and institutions at the hands of other national groups. How do I, in love, meet such needs? Whatever may be the case in some other world, the answer for this world is clear. Moved by love, I will work for a social structure, including legal and police elements, without which these personal needs cannot be met. And if the policeman uses his club or his gun or the army moves into an area where order has broken down, shall we say that this has nothing of love in it? Is it not plain that to stand aside from force is sometimes to turn our backs on indubitable human needs? It cannot be true to say that as soon as coercion enters, love departs.

Here I would like to make one final point: Christians—and moral men generally—will try in every possible way to build intelligence and character, inculcate good motives, increase voluntary cooperation for the common good. They will resist any tendency to give force the dominant role in domestic or international relationships. They will not, however, dismiss force as immoral or unchristian or unnecessary, but will accept it as having under love an indispensable function in human affairs.

THE ROOTS OF CHRISTIAN SOCIAL ACTION

Chapter Ten, *Man's New Home*

When Christian ministers and Christian churches talk and write about such things as intergovernmental economic aid, international trade, and international political organizations, they are still considered by some people to have left their proper business for excursions into fields in which they have neither responsibility nor competence.

As to the charge of incompetence, it must be admitted that it has more than a little justification. Churchmen have often made plain fools of themselves when they attempted to give advice to statesmen. Too often such advice has been based on sketchy information and superficial investigation. The well-meant admonition to work harder for peace or to put principles before expediency has not been very helpful. The government officer who receives such an admonition is probably trying as hard as any preacher or lay church leader to do the right thing. He may indeed need help from those whose central concern is with the ethical and moral aspects of public issues, but too often the advice offered is of no value because it seems to assume that if only the politician were guided by a sense of moral responsibility he could do what the churchman considers desirable. If someone who has a deep moral concern, a good grasp of the facts, and some awareness of political realities would suggest to the politician how he might move from a clearly unsatisfactory state of affairs to something a little better, this would be helpful and usually welcome.

Happily, the gap between Christian good intentions and Christian competence in this area is being shortened. Among Protestants, Roman Catholics, and Jews, increasing numbers of ministers and lay leaders are submitting themselves to the discipline of careful study and investigation. There is much less tendency to indulge in self-satisfying but inconsequential pulpit thunder and more inclination to the hard thinking and consultation that are the prerequisites of actual progress. We are having today an increasing and encouraging interaction between churchmen and political scientists, historians, physical scientists, and especially the decision-makers in government. Taken as a whole, the churches still have a long way to go in the effort to make their faith relevant to the actualities of international relations. But no one acquainted with the best word being done by ecumenical and denominational leaders and agencies can any longer support the blanket charge that in this field Christians do not know what they are talking about.

The other charge that Christian ministers and churches should stick to the gospel and stay away from economic and political problems involves the whole approach and motivation of what we have learned to call Christian social action. At this point, therefore, let us deal with the more fundamental matter and think about the interpretation of the Christian faith that impels Christians to concern themselves in down-to-earth fashion with all kinds of social problems, including the nation's foreign policy.

Observing that Christian social action is still not fully accepted as a part of the Christian mission, still inadequately supported, one sometimes feels like crying out: Look! What's the matter with Christians that they are so often hesitant or apologetic about this, or even opposed to it? How is it possible to be glad for the gospel with its good news of the Word made flesh and dwelling among us in the common ways of life and yet want the church to remain apart in some vague spiritual realm?

Or look at Russia before the revolution. Plenty of churches, but no Christian social action. Look at Cuba before Castro. Churches all over the place. But almost no Christian social action. Look at Germany when Hitler was coming to power. Sermons? Lots of them. Worship and sacrament were not absent. But not enough understanding of the Christian's involvement in and responsibility for the social order. That was the tragic defect. The absence of a social action emphasis in many American churches gives us the spectacle of the preaching of love and brotherhood accompanied by gross discrimination against the Negro.

Wherever the fault may lie—and part of it lies in an inadequate interpretation and practice of social action by those who have been its exponents – it should now be accepted as simple fact that a church that rejects social action is losing an important part of its usefulness to God and to hard-pressed humanity. Persons who care about human welfare should not be asked to support such a church.

To see what might justify such a blunt statement, let us go over some old territory. The living and indestructible roots of Christian social action are these:

First, human beings are, according to the Christian faith, made in the image of God and nothing else on earth bears that image. No other religion has as its center such radical, exclusive concern for the person. "The sabbath was made for man," said Jesus. This means that a Christian keeps his eye steadily and everlastingly on what is happening to people. Economic orders, governments, political parties, laws, principles, traditions, ways of life, science, schools, churches—none of these can claim priority or any kind of finality. They are made for man. They are to be honored when they serve man and changed or discarded when their service is defective. The worth of the person is the first and revolutionary Christian fact or principle. That worth is given by God. Everything else is subsidiary.

Second, love for human beings is a cardinal Christian obligation. This love is not mere sentimentality. It is not a simple romantic emotion. Christian love is serious loyalty to the being whom God made and for whom he gave his Son. The love we call Christian is serious about respecting human life, insists on giving every life a chance for its greatest possible fulfillment, and fights against everything that is hostile to man as a child of God. Christian love has dignity and depth. It is as gentle as giving a refugee a home, as forceful as using the police power to compel a segregated university to respect the humanity of a Negro. It may be mild, it may be stern; it is always serious about recognizing divinely-given human worth.

Third, a person is by definition a social being. There is no personality apart from community. The community begins with the family, branches out to the neighborhood, the town, the nation and the world. The community that cradles the individual, supports him, hurts him, helps him, and literally makes him possible includes agriculture and industry, the schools, the medical system, art, science, the church, citizens' organizations, and government. The only way of life as objectively absurd and dangerous as the totalitarianism that buries the individual in the mass is the individualism that tries to set him apart from the community. August Heckscher has summed up this truth in a flashing sentence: "A man's independence comes not from being falsely apart, but from being in a meaningful relation with others."

Fourth, man is, in the Christian understanding, a physical being endowed with spirit. In dealing with him, you cannot tell where one aspect of his nature leaves off and the other begins. This means that a spiritualized religion is as much in error as a materialistic Marxism. It means that if one wants to serve man, he cannot operate merely in some so-called spiritual realm. Nobody lives there. The forms and structures of the community—the economic system, international affairs, politics, recreation, art, science laboratories—are the business of anyone who cares deeply about human life. "Spiritual religion" was, one suspects, invented by someone who wanted an excuse for not taking seriously the Christian obligation to love one's neighbor.

Fifth, the business of Christians is not to build an institution called "the church," but to liberate human life in all its aspects — liberate it from fear, selfhatred, a narrow self-love, and the fruitless search for meaning and worth and happiness apart from God and our neighbors. Those who see this and have taken at least some steps on the road of liberation are the church, even if they never go inside a building called a church. Christ, the great Liberator, is not inside an institution called the church, sitting in judgment on the world outside the church. The Liberator is in the world; and the church, like all other institutions, is judged by him. Christian social action knocks on the doors of our churches, inviting them out of their unchristian and sociologically absurd self-centeredness—out into the world where men and women are and where God is.

Sixth, the word *social* in "Christian social action" has two connotations. It points to a fact already discussed: that the individual does not, cannot, exist in isolation; his life consists of relationships. But the word also suggests that in a society of great power structures and of increasing interdependence, the individual who wants to help others must work in and through organizations —organizations such as the American Medical Association, the Association of University Professors, the Chamber of Commerce, the League of Women Voters, the political party, the labor union, the church, the social action agency.

If someone says, "But all our organizations, committees, and parties depend finally on individual character and competence," we must agree that this is true. But we must add immediately that competence cannot be acquired in privacy and that character expresses itself in social relationships. Good citizens are not created in a private, sheltered place and then invited to participate in social groupings. By himself, alone, an individual is not even a person. Consider, as a good example, the late Eleanor Roosevelt. Who questions her uniqueness or her integrity? She met suffering with courage, fame with modesty, criticism without rancor. Here was no mere cog in a wheel, no mere faceless part of the social mass. Here was an individual.

But note how her personal character made its impact upon the world. Such impact came not apart from but through loyal participation in many organizations and committees. She grew as she became involved in social action. She understood that effective action for a better world must be accomplished in cooperation with others. Working alone, the individual cannot hope to work with much effectiveness.

So whichever way you look at it, "social action" is an important term that points to more than a mere hobby or vagary. The foundations of Christian social action are deep in the Christian faith, in the nature of man, and in the facts of contemporary life.

That part of Christian mission we call social action is not to be equated with liberalism or conservatism, with socialism or capitalism, with any political party or social panacea. Its center of interests is not politics or an economic system or the nation or the social order. Its whole concern is with persons. And because it cares, first and last, about this man, this woman, this child — whatever the race, class, creed, or nationality — it summons us to act with and through all the relationships and institutions that form the environment within which the person exists.

* * *

In brief, Christian social action is Christian love of the neighbor—love that knows *what* a man is, serves him *where* he is, and is resolved that the social order and all its institutions shall contribute to his fulfillment.